MED　　　1

BEDE JARRETT, O.P., M.A.

Edited by Paul A. Böer, Sr.

VERITATIS SPLENDOR PUBLICATIONS
et cognoscetis veritatem et veritas liberabit vos (Jn 8:32)

MMXIV

AD MAJOREM DEI GLORIAM

CONTENTS

MEDIAEVAL SOCIALISM

By
BEDE JARRETT, O.P., M.A.

London: T. C. & E. C. Jack

67 Long Acre, W.C., and Edinburgh

New York: Dodge Publishing Co.

1915

MEDIAEVAL SOCIALISM

CHAPTER I
INTRODUCTION

The title of this book may not unnaturally provoke suspicion. After all, howsoever we define it, socialism is a modern thing, and dependent almost wholly on modern conditions. It is an economic theory which has been evolved under pressure of circumstances which are admittedly of no very long standing. How then, it may be asked, is it possible to find any real correspondence between theories of old time and those which have grown out of present-day conditions of life? Surely whatever analogy may be drawn between them must be based on likenesses which cannot be more than superficial.

The point of view implied in this question is being increasingly adopted by all scientific students of social and political opinions, and is most certainly correct. Speculation that is purely philosophic may indeed turn round upon itself. The views of Grecian metaphysicians may continue for ever to find enthusiastic adherents;

though even here, in the realm of purely abstract reasoning, the progressive development of science, of psychology, and kindred branches of knowledge cannot fail by its influence to modify the form and arrangement of thought. But in those purely positive sciences (if indeed sciences they can properly be called) which deal with the life of man and its organisation, the very principles and postulates will be found to need continual readjustment. For with man's life, social, political, economic, we are in contact with forces which are of necessity always in a state of flux. For example, the predominance of agriculture, or of manufacture, or of commerce in the life of the social group must materially alter the attitude of the statesman who is responsible for its fortunes; and the progress of the nation from one to another stage of her development often entails (by altering from one class to another the dominant position of power) the complete reversal of her traditional maxims of government. Human life is not static, but dynamic. Hence the theories weaved round it must themselves be subject to the law of continuous development.

It is obvious that this argument cannot be gainsaid; and yet at the same time we may not be in any way illogical in venturing on an inquiry as to whether, in centuries not wholly dissimilar from our own, the mind of man worked itself out along lines parallel in some degree to contemporary systems of thought. Man's life differs, yet are the categories which mould his ideas eternally the same.

But before we go on to consider some early aspects of socialism, we must first ascertain what socialism itself essentially implies. Already within the lifetime of the present generation the word has greatly enlarged the scope of its significance. Many who ten years ago would have objected to it as a name of ill-omen see in it now nothing which may not be harmonised with the most ordinary of political and social doctrines. It is hardly any longer the badge of a school. Yet it does retain at any rate the bias of a tendency. It suggests chiefly the transference of ownership in land and capital from private hands into their possession in some form or other by the society. The means of this transference, and the manner in which this social possession is to be maintained, are very widely debated, and need not here be determined; it is sufficient for the matter of this book to have it granted that in this lies the germ of the socialistic theory of the State.

Once more it must be admitted that the meaning of "private ownership" and "social possession" will vary exceedingly in each age. When private dominion has become exceedingly individual and practically absolute, the opposition between the two terms will necessarily be very sharp. But in those earlier stages of national and social evolution, when the community was still regarded as composed, not of persons, but of groups, the antagonism might be, in point of theory, extremely limited; and in concrete cases it might possibly be difficult to determine where one ended and the other began. Yet it is undeniable that socialism in itself need mean no more than the central principle of State-ownership of capital and land. Such a conception is consistent with much private property in other forms than land and capital, and will be worked out in detail differently by different minds. But it is the principle, the essence of it, which justifies any claims made to the use of the name. We may therefore fairly call those theories socialistic which are covered by this central doctrine, and disregard, as irrelevant to the nature of the term, all added peculiarities contributed by individuals who have joined their forces to the movement.

By socialistic theories of the Middle Ages, therefore, we mean no more than those theories which from time to time came to the surface of political and social speculation in the form of communism, or of some other way of bringing about the transference which we have just indicated. But before plunging into the tanglement of these rather complicated problems, it will make for clearness if we consider quite briefly the philosophic heritage of social teaching to which the Middle Ages succeeded.

The Fathers of the Church had found themselves confronted with difficulties of no mean subtlety. On the one hand, the teaching of the Scriptures forced upon them the religious truth of the essential equality of all human nature. Christianity was a standing protest against the exclusiveness of the Jewish faith, and demanded through the attendance at one altar the recognition of an absolute oneness of all its members. The Epistles of St. Paul, which were the most scientific defence of Christian doctrine, were continually insisting on the fact that for the new faith there was no real division between Greek or barbarian, bond or free. Yet, on the other hand, there were equally unequivocal expressions concerning the reverence and respect due to authority and governance. St. Peter had taught that honour should be paid to Caesar, when Caesar was no other than Nero. St. Paul had as clearly preached subjection to the higher powers. Yet at the same time we know that the Christian truth of the essential equality of the whole human race was by some so construed as to be incompatible with the notion of civil authority. How, then, was this paradox to be explained? If all were equal, what justification would there be for civil authority? If civil authority was to be upheld, wherein lay the meaning of St. Paul's many boasts of the new levelling spirit of the Christian religion? The paradox was further complicated by two other problems. The question of the authority of the Imperial Government was found to be cognate with the questions of the institution of slavery and of private property. Here were three concrete facts on which the Empire seemed to be based. What was to be the Christian attitude towards them?

After many attempted explanations, which were largely personal, and, therefore, may be neglected here, a general agreement was come to by the leading Christian teachers of East and West. This was based on a theological distinction between human nature as it existed on its first creation, and then as it became in the state to which it was reduced after the fall of Adam. Created in original justice, as the phrase ran, the powers of man's soul were in perfect harmony. His sensitive nature, i.e. his passions, were in subjection to his will, his will to his reason, his reason to God. Had man continued in this state of innocence, government, slavery, and private property would never have been required. But Adam fell, and in his fall, said these Christian doctors, the whole conditions of his being were disturbed. The passions broke loose, and by their violence not unfrequently subjected the will to their dictatorship; together with the will they obscured and prejudiced the reason, which under their compulsion was no longer content to follow the Divine Reason or the Eternal Law of God. In a word, where order had previously reigned, a state of lawlessness now set in. Greed, lust for power, the spirit of insubordination, weakness of will, feebleness of mind, ignorance, all swarmed into the soul of man, and disturbed not merely the internal economy of his being, but his relations also to his fellows. The sin of Cain is the social result of this personal upheaval.

Society then felt the evils which attended this new condition of things, and it was driven, according to this patristic idea, to search about for remedies in order to restrain the anarchy which threatened to overwhelm the very existence of the race. Hence was introduced first of all the notion of a civil authority. It was found that without it, to use a phrase which Hobbes indeed has immortalised, but which can be easily paralleled from the writings of St. Ambrose or St. Augustine, "life was nasty, brutish, and short." To this idea of authority, there was quickly added the kindred ideas of private property and slavery. These two were found equally necessary for the well-being of human society. For the family became a determined group in which the patriarch wielded absolute power; his authority could be effective only when it could be employed not only over his own household, but also against other households, and thus in defence of his own. Hence the family must have the exclusive right to certain things. If others objected, the sole arbitrament was an appeal to force, and then the vanquished not only relinquished their claims to the objects in dispute, but became the slaves of those to whom they had previously stood in the position of equality and rivalry.

Thus do the Fathers of the Church justify these three institutions. They are all the result of the Fall, and result from sin. Incidentally it may be added that much of the language in which Hildebrand and others spoke of the civil power as "from the devil" is traceable to this theological concept of the history of its origin, and much of their hard language means no more than this. Private property, therefore, is due to the Fall, and becomes a necessity because of the presence of sin in the world.

But it is not only from the Fathers of the Church that the mediaeval tradition drew its force. For parallel with this patristic explanation came another, which was inherited from the imperial legalists. It was based upon a curious fact in the evolution of Roman law, which must now be shortly described.

For the administration of justice in Rome two officials were chosen, who between them disposed of all the cases in dispute. One, the Praetor Urbanus, concerned himself in all litigation between Roman citizens; the other, the Praetor Peregrinus, had his power limited to those matters only in which foreigners were involved; for the growth of the Roman Imperium had meant the inclusion of many under its suzerainty who could not boast technical citizenship. The Praetor Urbanus was guided in his decisions by the codified law of Rome; but the Praetor Peregrinus was in a very different position. He was left almost entirely to his own resources. Hence it was customary for him, on his assumption of office, to publish a list of the principles by which he intended to settle all the disputes between foreigners that were brought to his court. But on what foundation could his declaratory act be based? He was supposed to have previously consulted the particular laws of as many foreign nations as was possible, and to have selected from among them those which were found to be held in common by a number of tribes. The fact of this consensus to certain laws on the part of different races was supposed to imply that these were fragments of some larger whole, which came eventually to be called indifferently the

Law of Nature, or the Law of Nations. For at almost the very date when this Law of Nations was beginning thus to be built up, the Greek notion of one supreme law, which governed the whole race and dated from the lost Golden Age, came to the knowledge of the lawyers of Rome. They proceeded to identify the two really different concepts, and evolved for themselves the final notion of a fundamental rule, essential to all moral action. In time, therefore, this supposed Natural Law, from its venerable antiquity and universal acceptance, acquired an added sanction and actually began to be held in greater respect than even the declared law of Rome. The very name of Nature seemed to bring with it greater dignity. But at the same time it was carefully explained that this Lex Naturae was not absolutely inviolable, for its more accurate description was Lex or Jus Gentium. That is to say, it was not to be considered as a primitive law which lay embedded like first principles in human nature; but that it was what the nations had derived from primitive principles, not by any force of logic, but by the simple evolution of life. The human race had found by experience that the observance of the natural law entailed as a direct consequence the establishment of certain institutions. The authority, therefore, which these could boast was due to nothing more than the simple struggle for existence. Among these institutions were those same three (civil authority, slavery, private property), which the Fathers had come to justify by so different a method of argument. Thus, by the late Roman lawyers private property was upheld on the grounds that it had been found necessary by the human race in its advance along the road of life. To our modern ways of thinking it seems as though they had almost stumbled upon the theory of evolution, the gradual unfolding of social and moral perfection due to the constant pressure of circumstances, and the ultimate survival of what was most fit to survive. It was almost by a principle of natural selection that mankind was supposed to have determined the necessity of civil authority, slavery, private property, and the rest. The pragmatic test of life had been applied and had proved their need.

A third powerful influence in the development of Christian social teaching must be added to the others in order the better to grasp the mental attitude of the mediaeval thinkers. This was the rise and growth of monasticism. Its early history has been obscured by much legendary detail; but there is sufficient evidence to trace it back far into the beginnings of Christianity. Later there had come the stampede into the Thebaid, where both hermit life and the gathering together of many into a community seem to have been equally allowed as methods of asceticism. But by the fifth century, in the East and the West the movement had been effectively organised. First there was the canonical theory of life, introduced by St. Augustine. Then St. Basil and St. Benedict composed their Rules of Life, though St. Benedict disclaimed any idea of being original or of having begun something new. Yet, as a matter of fact, he, even more efficiently than St. Basil, had really introduced a new force into Christendom, and thereby became the undoubted father of Western monasticism.

Now this monasticism had for its primary intention the contemplation of God. In order to attain this object more perfectly, certain subsidiary observances were considered necessary. Their declared purpose was only to make contemplation easier; and they were never looked upon as essential to the monastic profession, but only as helps to its better working. Among these safeguards of monastic peace was included the removal of all anxieties concerning material well-being. Personal poverty--that is, the surrender of all personal claim to things the care of which might break in upon the fixed contemplation of God--was regarded as equally important for this purpose as obedience, chastity, and the continued residence in a certain spot. It had indeed been preached as a counsel of perfection by Christ Himself in His advice to the rich young man, and its significance was now very powerfully set forth by the Benedictine and other monastic establishments.

It is obvious that the existence of institutions of this kind was bound to exercise an influence upon Christian thought. It could not but be noticed that certain individual characters, many of whom claimed the respect of their generation, treated material possessions as hindrances to spiritual perfection. Through their example private property was forsworn, and community of possession became prominently put forward as being more in accordance with the spirit of Christ, who had lived with His Apostles, it was declared, out of the proceeds of a common purse. The result, from the point of view of the social theorists of the day, was to confirm the impression that private property was not a thing of much sanctity. Already, as we have seen, the Fathers had been brought to look at it as something sinful in its origin, in that the need of it was due entirely to the fall of our first parents. Then the legalists of Rome had brought to this the further consideration that mere expedience, universal indeed, but of no moral sanction, had dictated its institution as the only way to avoid continual strife among neighbours. And now the whole force of the religious ideals of the time was thrown in the same balance. Eastern and Western monasticism seemed to teach the same lesson, that private property was not in any sense a sacred thing. Rather it seemed to be an obstacle to the perfect devotion of man's being to God; and community of possession and life began to boast itself to be the more excellent following of Christ.

Finally it may be asserted that the social concept of feudalism lent itself to the teaching of the same lesson. For by it society was organised upon a system of land tenure whereby each held what was his of one higher than he, and was himself responsible for those beneath him in the social scale. Landowners, therefore, in the modern sense of the term, had no existence-- there were only landholders. The idea of absolute dominion without condition and without definite duties could have occurred to none. Each lord held his estate in feud, and with a definite arrangement for participating in the administration of justice, in the deliberative assembly, and in the war bands of his chief, who in turn owed the same duties to the lord above him. Even the king, who stood at the apex of this pyramid, was supposed to be merely holding his power and his territorial domain as representing the nation. At his coronation he bound himself to observe certain duties as the condition of his royalty, and he had to proclaim his own acceptance of these conditions before he could be anointed and crowned as king. Did he break through his coronation-oath, then the pledge of loyalty made by the people was considered to be in consequence without any binding force, and his subjects were released from their obedience. In this way, then, also private property was not likely to be deemed equivalent to absolute possession. It was held conditionally, and was not unfrequently forfeited for offences against the feudal code. It carried with it burdens which made its holding irksome, especially for all those who stood at the bottom of the scale, and found that the terms of their possession were rigorously enforced against them. The death of the tenant and the inheriting of his effects by his eldest son was made the occasion for exactions by the superior lord; for to him belonged certain of the dead man's military accoutrements as pledges, open and manifest, of the continued supremacy to be exercised over the successor.

Thus the extremely individual ideas as regards the holding of land which are to-day so prevalent would then have been hardly understood. Every external authority, the whole trend of public opinion, the teaching of the Christian Fathers, the example of religious bodies, the inherited views that had come down to the later legalists from the digests of the imperial era, the basis of social order, all deflected the scale against the predominance of any view of land tenure or holding which made it an absolute and unrestricted possession. Yet at the same time, and for the same cause, the modern revolt against all individual possession would have been for the mediaeval theorists equally hard to understand. Absolute communism, or the idea of a State which under the magic of that abstract title could interfere with the whole social order, was too utterly foreign to their ways of thinking to have found a defender. The king they knew, and the people, and the Church; but the State (which the modern socialist invokes) would have been an unimaginable thing.

In that age, therefore, we must not expect to find any fully-fledged Socialism. We must be content to notice theories which are socialistic rather than socialist.

CHAPTER II
SOCIAL CONDITIONS

So long as a man is in perfect health, the movements of his life-organs are hardly perceptible to him. He becomes conscious of their existence only when something has happened to obstruct their free play. So, again, is it with the body politic, for just so long as things move easily and without friction, hardly are anyone's thoughts stimulated in the direction of social reform. But directly distress or disturbance begin to be felt, public attention is awakened, and directed to the consideration of actual conditions. Schemes are suggested, new ideas broached. Hence, that there were at all in the Middle Ages men with remedies to be applied to "the open sores of the world," makes us realise that there must have been in mediaeval life much matter for discontent. Perhaps not altogether unfortunately, the seeds of unrest never need much care in sowing, for the human heart would else advance but little towards "the perfect day." The rebels of history have been as necessary as the theorists and the statesmen; indeed, but for the rebels, the statesmen would probably have remained mere politicians.

Upon the ruins of the late Empire the
Germanic races built up their State. Out of the
fragments of the older villa they erected the
manor. No doubt this new social unit contained
the strata of many civilisations; but it will suffice
here to recognise that, while it is perhaps
impossible to apportion out to each its own
particular contribution to the whole result, the
manor must have been affected quite
considerably by Roman, Celt, and Teuton. The
chief difference which we notice between this
older system and the conditions of modern
agricultural life--for the manor was pre-
eminently a rural organism--lies in the
enormous part then played in the organisation
of society by the idea of Tenure. For, through
all Western civilisation, from the seventh
century to the fourteenth, the personal equation
was largely merged in the territorial. One and
all, master and man, lord and tenant, were "tied
to the soil." Within the manor there was first
the land held in demesne, the "in-land"--this
was the perquisite of the lord himself; it was
farmed by him directly. Only when modern
methods began to push out the old feudal
concepts do we find this portion of the estate
regularly let out to tenants, though there are

evidences of its occasionally having been done
even in the twelfth century. But besides what
belonged thus exclusively to the lord of the
manor, there was a great deal more that was
legally described as held in villeinage. That is to
say, it was in the hands of others, who had
conditional use of it. In England these tenants
were chiefly of three kinds--the villeins, the
cottiers, the serfs. The first held a house and
yard in the village street, and had in the great
arable fields that surrounded them strips of land
amounting sometimes to thirty acres. To their
lord they owed work for three days each week;
they also provided oxen for the plough. But
more than half of their time could be devoted
to the farming of their property. Then next in
order came the cottiers, whose holding
probably ran to not more than five acres. They
had no plough-work, and did more of the
manual labour of the farm, such as hedging,
nut-collecting, &c. A much greater portion of
their time than was the case with the villeins
was at the disposal of their master, nor indeed,
owing to the lesser extent of their property, did
they need so much opportunity for working
their own land. Lowest in the scale of all
(according to the Domesday Book of William I,

the first great land-value survey of all England,
they numbered not more than sixteen per cent.
of the whole population) came the slaves or
serfs. These had almost exclusively the live
stock to look after, being engaged as foresters,
shepherds, swineherds, and servants of the
household. They either lived under the lord's
own roof, or might even have their cottage in
the village with its strip of land about it,
sufficient, with the provisions and cloth
provided them, to eke out a scanty livelihood.
Distinct from these three classes and their
officials (bailiffs, seneschals, reeves, &c.) were
the free tenants, who did no regular work for
the manor, but could not leave or part with
their land. Their services were requisitioned at
certain periods like harvest-time, when there
came a demand for more than the ordinary
number of hands. This sort of labour was
known as boon-work.

It is clear at once that, theoretically at least,
there was no room in such a community for the
modern landless labourer. Where all the
workers were paid by their tenancy of land,
where, in other words, fixity and stability of
possession were the very basis of social life, the
fluidity of labour was impossible. Men could

not wander from place to place offering to
employers the hire of their toil. Yet we feel sure
that, in actual fact, wherever the population
increased, there must have grown up in the
process of time a number of persons who could
find neither work nor maintenance on their
father's property. Younger sons, or more
remote descendants, must gradually have found
that there was no scope for them, unless, like an
artisan class, they worked for wages. Exactly at
what date began the rise of this agricultural and
industrial class of fee labourers we cannot very
clearly tell. But in England--and probably the
same holds good elsewhere--between 1200 and
1350 there are traces of its great development.
There is evidence, which each year becomes
more ample and more definite, that during that
period there was an increasingly large number
of people pressing on the means of subsistence.
Though the land itself might be capable of
supporting a far greater number of inhabitants,
the part under cultivation could only just have
been enough to keep the actually existing
population from the margin of destitution. The
statutes in English law which protest against a
wholesale occupation of the common-land by
individuals were not directed merely against the

practices of a landlord class, for the makers of
the law were themselves landlords. It is far
more likely that this invasion of village rights
was due to the action of these "landless men,"
who could not otherwise be accommodated.
The superfluous population was endeavouring
to find for itself local maintenance.

Precisely at this time, too, in England--where
the steps in the evolution from mediaeval to
modern conditions have been more clearly
worked out than elsewhere--increase of trade
helped to further the same development.
Money, species, in greater abundance was
coming into circulation. The traders were
beginning to take their place in the national life.
The Guilds were springing into power, and
endeavouring to capture the machinery of
municipal government. As a result of all this
commercial activity money payments became
more frequent. The villein was able to pay his
lord instead of working for him, and by the sale
of the produce from his own yard-land was put
in a position to hire helpers for himself, and to
develop his own agricultural resources. Nor was
it the tenant alone who stood to gain by this
arrangement. The lord, too, was glad of being
possessed of money. He, too, needed it as a

substitute for his duty of military service to the king, for scutage (the payment of a tax graduated according to the number of knights, which each baron had to lead personally in time of war as a condition of holding land at all) had taken the place of the old feudal levy. Moreover, he was probably glad to obtain hired labour in exchange for the forced labour which the system of tenure made general; just as later the abolition of slavery was due largely to the fact that, in the long run, it did not pay to have the plantations worked by men whose every advantage it was to shirk as much toil as possible.

But in most cases, as far as can be judged now, the lord was methodical in releasing services due to him. The week-work was first and freely commuted, for regular hired labour was easy to obtain; but the boon-work--the work, that is, which was required for unusual circumstances of a purely temporary character (such as harvesting, &c.)--was, owing to the obvious difficulty of its being otherwise supplied, only arranged for in the last resort. Thus, by one of the many paradoxes of history, the freest of all tenants were the last to achieve freedom. When the serfs had been set at liberty by manumission, the socage-tenants or free-tenants, as they were called, were still bound by their fixed agreements of tenure. It is evident, however, that such emancipation as did take place was conditioned by the supply of free labour, primarily, that is, by the rising surplus of population. Not until he was certain of being able to hire other labourers would a landholder let his own tenants slip off the burdens of their service.

But this process, by which labour was rendered less stationary, was immeasurably hastened by the advent of a terrible catastrophe. In 1347 the Black Death arrived from the East. Across Europe it moved, striking fear by the inevitableness of its coming. It travelled at a steady rate, so that its arrival could be easily foretold. Then, too, the unmistakable nature of its symptoms and the suddenness of the death it caused also added to the horror of its approach.

On August 15, 1349, it got to Bristol, and by Michaelmas had reached London. For a year or more it ravaged the countryside, so that whole villages were left without inhabitants. Seeing England so stunned by the blow, the Scots prepared to attack, thinking the moment propitious for paying off old scores; but their army, too, was smitten by the pestilence, and their forces broke up. Into every glen of Wales it worked its havoc; in Ireland only the English were affected--the "wild Irish" were immune. But in 1357 even these began to suffer. Curiously enough, Geoffrey Baker in his Chronicle (which, written in his own hand, after six hundred years yet remains in the Bodleian at Oxford) tells us that none fell till they were afraid of it. Still more curiously, Chaucer, Langland, and Wycliff, who all witnessed it, hardly mention it at all. There could not be any more eloquent tribute to the nameless horror that it caused than this hushed silence on the part of three of England's greatest writers.

Henry Knighton of Leicester Abbey, canon and chronicler, tells us some of the consequences following on the plague, and shows us very clearly the social upheaval it effected. The population had now so much diminished that prices of live stock went down, an ox costing 4s., a cow 12d., and a sheep 3d. But for the same reason wages went up, for labour had suddenly grown scarce. For want of hands to bring in the harvest, whole crops rotted in the fields. Many a manor had lost a third of its inhabitants, and it was difficult, under the fixed services of land tenure, to see what remedy could be applied. In despair the feudal system was set aside, and lord competed with lord to obtain landless labourers, or to entice within their jurisdiction those whose own masters ill-treated them in any way. The villeins themselves sought to procure enfranchisement, and the right to hire themselves out to their lords, or to any master they might choose. Commutation was not particularly in evidence as the legal method of redress; though it too was no doubt here and there arranged for. But for the most part the villein took the law into his own hands, left his manor, and openly sold his labour to the highest bidder.

But at once the governing class took fright. In their eyes it seemed as though their tenants were taking an unfair advantage of the disorganisation of the national life. Even before Parliament could meet, in 1349 an ordnance was issued by the King (Edward III), which compelled all servants, whether bond or free, to take up again the customary services, and forced work on all who had no income in land, or were not otherwise engaged. The lord on whose manor the tenant had heretofore dwelt had preferential claim to his labour, and could threaten with imprisonment every refractory villein. Within two years a statute had been enacted by Parliament which was far more detailed in its operation, fixing wages at the rate they had been in the twentieth year of the King's reign (i.e. at a period before the plague, when labour was plentiful), and also with all appearance of justice determining the prices of agricultural produce. It was the first of a very long series of Acts of Parliament that, with every right intention, but with a really obvious futility, endeavoured to reduce everything to what it had been in the past, to put back the hands of the clock, and keep them back. But one strange fact is noticeable.

Whether unconsciously or not, the framers of these statutes were themselves striking the hardest blow at the old system of tenure. From 1351 the masters' preferential claim to the villeins of their own manor disappears, or is greatly limited. Henceforth the labourers are to appear in the market place with their tools, and (reminiscent of scriptural conditions) wait till some man hired them. The State, not the lord, is now regulating labour. Labour itself has passed from being "tied to the soil," and has become fluid. It is no longer a personal obligation, but a commodity.

Even Parliament recognised that in many respects at least the old order had passed away. The statute of 1351 allows "men of the counties of Stafford, Lancaster, Derby, the borders of Wales and Scotland, &c., to come in August time to labour in other counties, and to return in safety, as they were heretofore wont to do." It is the legalisation of what had been looked at, up till then, askance. The long, silent revolution had become conscious. But the lords were, as we have said, not altogether sorry for the turn things had taken. Groaning under pressure from the King's heavy war taxation, and under the demands which the advance of new standards of comfort (especially between 1370 and 1400) entailed, they let off on lease even the demesne land, and became to a very great extent mere rent-collectors. Commutation proceeded steadily, with much haggling so as to obtain the highest price from the eager tenant. Wages rose slowly, it is true, but rose all the same; and rent, though still high, was becoming, on the whole, less intolerable.

But the drain of the French war, and the peculation in public funds brought about the final upheaval which completed what the Black Death had begun. The capricious and unfairly graduated poll-tax of 1381 came as a climax, and roused the Great Revolt of that year, a revolt carefully engineered and cleverly organised, which yet for the demands it made is a striking testimony to the moderation, the good sense, and also the oppressed state of the English peasant.

The fourfold petition presented to the King by the rebels was:

(1) The abolition of serfdom.

(2) The reduction of rent to 4d. per acre.

(3) The liberty to buy and sell in market.

(4) A free pardon.

Compare the studiously restrained tone of these articles with the terrible atrocities and vengeance wreaked by the Jacquerie in France, and the no less awful mob violence perpetrated in Florence by the Ciompi. While it shows no doubt in a kindly light the more equitable rule of the English landholder, it remains a monument, also, of the fair-mindedness of the English worker.

In the towns much the same sort of struggle had been going on; for the towns themselves, more often than not, sprang up on the demesne of some lord, whether king, Church, or baron. But here the difficulties were complicated still further by the interference of the Guilds, which in the various trades regulated the hours of labour, the quality of the work, and the rate of remuneration. Yet, on the other hand, it is undoubted that, once the squalor of the earlier stages of urban life had been removed or at least improved, the social condition of the poor, from the fourteenth century onwards, was immeasurably superior in the towns to what it was in the country districts.

The quickening influence of trade was making itself felt everywhere. In 1331 the cloth trade was introduced at Bristol, and settled down then definitely in the west of England. In the north we notice the beginnings of the coal trade. Licence was given to the burgesses of Newcastle to dig for coal in 1351; and in 1368 two merchants of the same city had applied for and obtained royal permission to send that precious commodity "to any part of the kingdom, either by land or water." Even vast speculations were opening up for English commercial enterprise, when, by cornering the wool and bribing the King, a ring of merchants were able to break the Italian banking houses, and disorganise the European money market, for on the Continent all this energy in trade was already old. The house of Anjou, for example, had made the kingdom of Naples a great trading centre. Its corn and cattle were famous the world over. But in Naples it was the sovereigns (like Edward III and Edward IV in England) who patronised the commercial instincts of their people. By the indefatigable genius of the royal house, industry was stimulated, and private enterprise encouraged. By wise legislation the interests of the merchants were safeguarded; and by the personal supervision of Government, fiscal duties were moderated, the currency kept pure and stable, weights and measures reduced to uniformity, the ease and security of communications secured.

No doubt trade not seldom, even in that age, led to much evil. Parliament in England raised its voice against the trickery and deceit practised by the greater merchants towards the small shopkeepers, and complained bitterly of the growing custom of the King to farm out to the wealthier among them the subsidies and port-duties of the kingdom. For the whole force of the break-up of feudal conditions was to turn the direction of power into the hands of a small, but moneyed class. Under Edward III there is a distinct appearance of a set of nouveaux riches, who rise to great prominence and take their places beside the old landed nobility. De la Pole, the man who did most to establish the prosperity of Hull, is an excellent example of what is often thought to be a decidedly modern type. He introduced bricks from the Low Countries, and apparently by this means and some curious banking speculations of very doubtful honesty achieved a great fortune. The King paid a visit to his country house, and made him Chief Baron of the Exchequer, in which office he was strongly suspected of not always passing to the right quarter some of the royal moneys. His son became Earl of Suffolk and Lord Chancellor; and a marriage with royalty made descendants of the family on more than one occasion heirs-at-law of the Crown.

Even the peasant was beginning to feel the amelioration of his lot, found life easy, and work something to be shirked. In his food, he was starting to be delicate. Says Langland in his "Vision of Piers Plowman":

"Then labourers landless that lived by their hands,   Would deign not to dine upon worts a day old.   No penny-ale pleased them, no piece of good bacon,   Only fresh flesh or fish, well-fried or well-baked,   Ever hot and still hotter to heat well their maw."

And he speaks elsewhere of their laziness:

"Bewailing his lot as a workman to live, He grumbles against God and grieves without reason,   And curses the king and his council after   Who licence the laws that the labourers grieve."

That the poor could thus become fastidious was a good sign of the rising standard of comfort.

But for all that life was hard, and much at the mercy of the weather, and of the assaults of man's own fellows. The houses of the better folk were of brick and stone, and glass windows were just becoming known, whereas the substitute of oiled paper had been neither cheerful nor of very much protection. But the huts of the poor were of plastered mud; and even the walls of a quite respectable man's abode, we know from one court summons to have been pierced by arrows shot at him by a pugnacious neighbour. The plaintiff offered to take judge and jury then and there and show them these "horrid weapons" still sticking to the exterior. In the larger houses the hall had branched off, by the fourteenth century, into withdrawing-rooms, and parlours, and bedrooms, such as the Paston Letters describe with much curious wealth of detail. Lady Milicent Falstolf, we are told, was the only one in her father's household who had a ewer and washing-basin.

Yet with all the lack of the modern necessities of life, human nature was still much the same. The antagonism between rich and poor, which the collapse of feudal relations had strained to breaking-point, was not perhaps normally so intense as it is to-day; yet there was certainly much oppression and unnecessary hardships to be suffered by the weak, even in that age. The Ancren Riwle, that quaint form of life for ankeresses drawn up by a Dominican in the thirteenth century, shows that even then, despite the distance of years and the passing of so many generations, the manners and ways and mental attitudes of people depended very much as to whether they were among those who had, or who had not; the pious author in one passage of homely wit compares certain of the sisters to "those artful children of rich parents who purposely tear their clothes that they may have new ones."

There have always been wanton waste and destitution side by side; and on the prophecy of the One to whom all things were revealed, we know that the poor shall be always with us. Yet we must honour those who, like their Master, strive to smooth away the anxious wrinkles of the world.

CHAPTER III
THE COMMUNISTS

There have always been religious teachers for whom all material creation was a thing of evil. Through the whole of the Middle Ages, under the various names of Manicheans, Albigensians, Vaudois, &c., they became exceedingly vigorous, though their importance was only fitful. For them property was essentially unclean, something to be avoided as carrying with it the in-dwelling of the spirit of evil. Etienne de Bourbon, a Dominican preacher of the thirteenth century, who got into communication with one of these strange religionists, has left us a record, exceedingly unprejudiced, of their beliefs. And amongst their other tenets, he mentions this, that they condemned all who held landed property. It will be here noticed that as regards these Vaudois (or Poor Men of Lyons, as he informs us they were called), there could have been no question of communism at all, for a common holding of property would have been as objectionable as private property. To hold material things either in community or severalty was in either case to bind oneself to the evil principle. Yet Etienne tells us that there was a sect among them which did sanction communism; they were called, in fact, the Communati (Tractatus de Diversis Materiis Predicabilibus, Paris, 1877, p. 281). How they were able to reconcile this social state with their beliefs it is quite impossible to say; but the presumption is that the example of the early Christians was cited as of sufficient authority by some of these teachers. Certain it is that a sect still lingered on into the thirteenth century, called the Apostolici, who clung to the system which had been in vogue among the Apostles. St. Thomas Aquinas (Summa Theologica, 2a, 2ae, 66, 2) mentions them, and quotes St. Augustine as one who had already refuted them. But these were seemingly a Christian body, whereas the Albigensians could hardly make any such claim, since they repudiated any belief in Christ's humanity, for it conflicted with their most central dogma.

Still it is clear that there were in existence certain obscure bodies which clung to communism. The published records of the Inquisition refer incessantly to preachers of this kind who denied private property, asserted that no rich man could get to heaven, and attacked the practice of almsgiving as something utterly immoral.

The relation between these teachers and the
Orders of friars has never been adequately
investigated. We know that the Dominicans and
Franciscans were from their earliest institution
sent against them, and must therefore have
been well acquainted with their errors. And, as a
fact, we find rising among the friars a party
which seemed no little infected with the
"spiritual" tendency of these very Vaudois. The
Franciscan reverence for poverty, which the
Poor Man of Assisi had so strenuously
advocated, had in fact become almost a
superstition. Instead of being, as the saint had
intended it to be, merely a means to an end, it
had in process of time become looked upon as
the essential of religion. When, therefore, the
excessive adoption of it made religious life an
almost impossible thing, an influential party
among the Franciscans endeavoured to have
certain modifications made which should limit it
within reasonable bounds. But opposed to them
was a determined, resolute minority, which
vigorously refused to have any part in such
"relaxations." The dispute between these two
branches of the Order became at last so
tempestuous that it was carried to the Pope,
who appointed a commission of cardinals and

theologians to adjudicate on the rival theories. Their award was naturally in favour of those who, by their reasonable interpretation of the meaning of poverty, were fighting for the efficiency of their Order. But this drove the extreme party into still further extremes. They rejected at once all papal right to interfere with the constitutions of the friars, and declared that only St. Francis could undo what St. Francis himself had bound up. Nor was this all, for in the pursuance of their zeal for poverty they passed quickly from denunciations of the Pope and the wealthy clergy (in which their rhetoric found very effective matter for argument) into abstract reasoning on the whole question of the private possession of property. The treatises which they have left in crabbed Latin and involved methods of argument make wearisome and irritating reading. Most are exceedingly prolix. After pages of profound disquisitions, the conclusions reached seem to have advanced the problem no further. Yet the gist of the whole is certainly an attempt to deny to any Christian the right to temporal possessions. Michael of Cesena, the most logical and most effective of the whole group, who eventually became the Minister-General of this portion of the Order, does not hesitate to affirm the incompatibility of Christianity and private property. From being a question as to the teaching of St. Francis, the matter had grown to one as to the teaching of Christ; and in order to prove satisfactorily that the practice of poverty as inculcated by St. Francis was absolute and inviolable, it was found necessary to hold that it was equally the declared doctrine of Christ.

Even Ockham, a brilliant Oxford Franciscan, who, together with Michael, defended the Emperor, Louis of Bavaria, in his struggle against Pope John XXII, let fall in the heat of controversy some sayings which must have puzzled his august patron; for Louis would have been the very last person for whom communism had any charms. Closely allied in spirit with these "Spiritual Franciscans," as they were called, or Fraticelli, were those curious mediaeval bodies of Beguins and Beghards. Hopelessly pantheistic in their notion of the Divine Being, and following most peculiar methods of reaching on earth the Beatific Vision, they took up with the same doctrine of the religious duty of the communistic life. They declared the practice of holding private property to be contrary to the Divine Law.

Another preacher of communism, and one whose name is well known for the active propaganda of his opinions, and for his share in the English Peasant Revolt of 1381, was John Ball, known to history as "The Mad Priest of Kent." There is some difficulty in finding out what his real theories were, for his chroniclers were his enemies, who took no very elaborate steps to ascertain the exact truth about him. Of course there is the famous couplet which is said to have been the text of all his sermons:

"Whaune Adam dalf and Eve span,   Who was thane a gentilman?"[1]

at least, so it is reported of him in the Chronicon Angliae, the work of an unknown monk of St. Albans (Roll Series, 1874, London, p. 321). Froissart, that picturesque journalist, who naturally, as a friend of the Court, detested the levelling doctrines of this political rebel, gives what he calls one of John Ball's customary sermons. He is evidently not attempting to report any actual sermon, but rather to give a general summary of what was supposed to be Ball's opinions. As such, it is worth quoting in full.

"My good friends, things cannot go on well in England, nor ever will until everything shall be in common; when there shall be neither vassal nor lord, and all distinctions levelled; when lords shall be no more masters than ourselves. How ill have they used us! and for what reason do they thus hold us in bondage? Are we not all descended from the same parents--Adam and Eve? And what can they show, and what reason give, why they should be more the masters than ourselves? Except, perhaps, in making us labour and work for them to spend." Froissart goes on to say that for speeches of this nature the Archbishop of Canterbury put Ball in prison, and adds that for himself he considers that "it would have been better if he had been confined there all his life, or had been put to death." However, the Archbishop "set him at liberty, for he could not for conscience sake have put him to death" (Froissart's Chronicle, 1848, London, book ii. cap. 73, pp. 652-653).

From this extract all that can be gathered with certainty is the popular idea of the opinions John Ball held; and it is instructive to find that in the Primate's eyes there was nothing in the doctrine to warrant the extreme penalty of the law. But in reality we have no certainty as to what Ball actually taught, for in another account we find that, preaching on Corpus Christi Day, June 13, 1381, during the last days of the revolt, far fiercer words are ascribed to him. He is made to appeal to the people to destroy the evil lords and unjust judges, who lurked like tares among the wheat. "For when the great ones have been rooted up and cast away, all will enjoy equal freedom--all will have common nobility, rank, and power." Of course it may be that the war-fever of the revolt had affected his language; but the sudden change of tone imputed in the later speeches makes the reader somewhat suspicious of the authenticity.

The same difficulty which is experienced in discovering the real mind of Ball is encountered when dealing with Wat Tyler and Jack Straw, who were, with him, the leaders of the revolt. The confession of Jack Straw quoted in the Chronicon Angliae, like nearly all mediaeval "confessions," cannot be taken seriously. His accusers and judges readily supplied what they considered he should have himself admitted. Without any better evidence we cannot with safety say along what lines he pushed his theories, or whether, indeed, he had any theories at all. Again, Wat Tyler is reported to have spoken threateningly to the King on the morning of his murder by Lord Mayor Walworth; but the evidence is once more entirely one-sided, contributed by those who were only too anxious to produce information which should blacken the rebels in the minds of the educated classes. As a matter of fact, the purely official documents, in which we can probably put much more reliance (such as the petitions that poured in from all parts of the country on behalf of the peasants, and the proclamations issued by Richard II, in which all their demands were granted on condition of their immediate withdrawal from the capital), do not leave the impression that the people really advocated any communistic doctrines; oppression is complained of, the lawyers execrated, the labour laws are denounced, and that is practically all.

It may be, indeed, that the traditional view of Ball and his followers, which makes them one with the contemporaneous revolts of the Jacquerie in France, the Ciompi in Florence, &c., has some basis in fact. But at present we have no means of gauging the precise amount of truth it contains.

But even better known than John Ball is one who is commonly connected with the Peasant Revolt, and whose social opinions are often grouped under the same heading as that of the "Mad Priest of Kent,"--John Wycliff, Master of Balliol, and parson of Lutterworth. This Oxford professor has left us a number of works from which to quarry materials to build up afresh the edifice he intended to erect. His chief contribution is contained in his De Civili Dominio, but its composition extended over a long period of years, during which time his views were evidently changing; so that the precise meaning of his famous theory on the Dominion of Grace is therefore difficult to ascertain.

But in the opening of his treatise he lays down the two main "truths" upon which his whole system rests:

I. No one in mortal sin has any right to the gifts of God;

II. Whoever is in a state of grace has a right, not indeed to   possess the good things of God, but to use them.

He seems to look upon the whole question from a feudal point of view. Sin is treason, involving therefore the forfeiture of all that is held of God. Grace, on the other hand, makes us the liegemen of God, and gives us the only possible right to all His good gifts. But, he would seem to argue, it is incontestable that property and power are from God, for so Scripture plainly assures us. Therefore, he concludes, by grace, and grace alone, are we put in dominion over all things; once we are in loyal subjection to God, we own all things, and hold them by the only sure title. "Dominion by grace" is thus made to lead direct to communism. His conclusion is quite clear: Omnia debent esse communia.

In one of his sermons (Oxford, 1869, vol. i. p. 260), when he has proved this point with much complacent argumentation, he poses himself with the obvious difficulty that in point of fact this is not true; for many who are apparently in mortal sin do possess property and have dominion. What, then, is to be done, for "they be commonly mighty, and no man dare take from them"? His answer is not very cheerful, for he has to console his questioner with the barren scholastic comfort that "nevertheless, he hath them not, but occupieth things that be not his." Emboldened by the virtue of this dry logic, he breaks out into his gospel of plain assertion that "the saints have now all things that they would have." His whole argument, accordingly, does not get very far, for he is still speaking really (though he does not at times very clearly distinguish between the two) much more about the right to a thing than its actual possession. He does not really defend the despoiling of the evil rich at all--in his own graphic phrase, "God must serve the Devil"; and all that the blameless poor can do is to say to themselves that though the rich "possess" or "occupy," the poor "have." It seems a strange sort of "having"; but he is careful to note that, "as philosophers say, 'having is in many manners.'"

Wycliff himself, perhaps, had not definitely made up his mind as to the real significance of his teaching; for the system which he sketches does not seem to have been clearly thought out. His words certainly appear to bear a communistic sense; but it is quite plain that this was not the intention of the writer. He defends Plato at some length against the criticism of Aristotle, but only on the ground that the disciple misunderstood the master: "for I do not think Socrates to have so intended, but only to have had the true catholic idea that each should have the use of what belongs to his brother" (De Civili Dominio, London, 1884-1904, vol. i. p. 99). And just a few lines farther on he adds, "But whether Socrates understood this or not, I shall not further question. This only I know, that by the law of charity every Christian ought to have the just use of what belongs to his neighbour." What else is this really but the teaching of Aristotle that there should be "private property and common use"? It is, in fact, the very antithesis of communism.

Some have thought that he was fettered in his language by his academic position; but no Oxford don has ever said such hard things about his Alma Mater as did this master of Balliol. "Universities," says he, "houses of study, colleges, as well as degrees and masterships in them, are vanities introduced by the heathen, and profit the Church as little and as much as does Satan himself." Surely it were impossible to accuse such a man of economy of language, and of being cowed by any University fetish.

His words, we have noted above, certainly can bear the interpretation of a very levelling philosophy. Even in his own generation he was accused through his followers of having had a hand in instigating the revolt. His reply was an angry expostulation (Trevelyan's England in the Age of Wycliff, 1909, London, p. 201). Indeed, considering that John of Gaunt was his best friend and protector, it would be foolish to connect Wycliff with the Peasant Rising. The insurgents, in their hatred of Gaunt, whom they looked upon as the cause of their oppression, made all whom they met swear to have no king named John (Chronicon Angliae, p. 286). And John Ball, whom the author of the Fasciculi Zizaniorum (p. 273, Roll Series, 1856, London) calls the "darling follower" of Wycliff, can only be considered as such in his doctrinal teaching on the dogma of the Real Presence. It must be remembered that to contemporary England Wycliff's fame came from two of his opinions, viz. his denial of a real objective Presence in the Mass (for Christ was there only by "ghostly wit"), and his advice to King and Parliament to confiscate Church lands. But whenever Ball or anyone else is accused of being a follower of Wycliff, nothing else is probably referred to than the professor's well-known opinion on the sacrament of the Eucharist. Hence it is that the

Chronicon Angliae speaks of John Ball as having been imprisoned earlier in life for his Wycliffite errors, which it calls simply perversa dogmata. The "Morning Star of the Reformation" being therefore declared innocent of complicity with the Peasant Revolt, it is interesting to note to whom it is that he ascribes the whole force of the rebellion. For him the head and front of all offending was the hated friars.

Against this imputation the four Orders of friars (the Dominicans, Franciscans, Augustinians, and Carmelites) issued a protest. Fortunately in their spirited reply they give the reasons on account of which they are supposed to have shared in the rising. These were principally negative. Thus it was stated that their influence with the people was so great that had they ventured to oppose the spirit of revolt their words would have been listened to (Fasciculi Zizaniorum, p. 293). The chronicler of St. Albans is equally convinced of their weakness in not preventing it, and declares that the flattery which they used alike on rich and poor had also no mean share in producing the social unrest (Chronicon Angliae, p. 312). Langland also, in his "Vision of Piers

Plowman," goes out of his way to denounce them for their levelling doctrines:

"Envy heard this and bade friars go to school,   And learn logic and law and eke contemplation,   And preach men of Plato and prove it by Seneca   That all things under Heaven ought to be in common,   And yet he lieth, as I live, and to the lewd so preacheth For God made to men a law and Moses it taught--

   Non concupisces rem proximi tui" (Thou shalt not covet thy neighbour's goods).

 Here then it is distinctly asserted that the spread of communistic doctrines was due to the friars. Moreover, the same popular opinion is reflected in the fabricated confession of Jack Straw, for he is made to declare that had the rebels been successful, all the monastic orders, as well as the secular clergy, would have been put to death, and only the friars would have been allowed to continue. Their numbers would have sufficed for the spiritual needs of the whole kingdom (Chronicon Angliae, p. 309). Moreover, it has been noticed that not a few of them actually took part in the revolt, heading some of the bands of countrymen who marched on London.

It will have been seen, therefore, that Communism was a favourite rallying-cry throughout the Middle Ages for all those on whom the oppression of the feudal yoke bore heavily. It was partly also a religious ideal for some of the strange gnostic sects which flourished at that era. Moreover, it was an efficient weapon when used as an accusation, for Wycliff and the friars alike both dreaded its imputation. Perhaps of all that period, John Ball alone held it consistently and without shame. Eloquent in the way of popular appeal, he manifestly endeavoured to force it as a social reform on the peasantry, who were suffering under the intolerable grievance of the Statutes of Labourers. But though he roused the countryside to his following, and made the people for the first time a thing of dread to nobles and King, it does not appear that his ideas spread much beyond his immediate lieutenants. Just as in their petitions the rebels made no doctrinal statements against Church teaching, nor any capital out of heretical attacks (except, singularly enough, to accuse the Primate, whom they subsequently put to death, of overmuch leniency to Lollards), so, too, they made no reference to the central idea of Ball's social theories. In fact, little abstract matter could well have appealed to them. Concrete oppression was all they knew, and were this done away with, it is evident that they would have been well content.

The case of the friars is curious. For though their superiors made many attempts to prove their hostility to the rebels, it is evident that their actual teaching was suspected by those in high places. It is the exact reversal of the case of Wycliff. His views, which sounded so favourable to communism, are found on examination to be really nothing but a plea to leave things alone, "for the saints have now all they would have"; while on the other hand the theories of the friars, in themselves so logical and consistent, and in appearance obviously conservative to the fullest extent, turn out to contain the germ of revolution.

Said Lord Acton with his sober wit: "Not the devil, but St. Thomas Aquinas, was the first Whig."

FOOTNOTE:

[1] This rhyme is of course much older than
John Ball; cf. Richard Rolle (1300-1349), i. 73,
London, 1895.

Bede Jarrett, O.P., M.A.

CHAPTER IV
THE SCHOOLMEN

The schoolmen in their adventurous quest after a complete harmony of all philosophic learning could not neglect the great outstanding problems of social and economic life. They flourished at the very period of European history when commerce and manufacture were coming back to the West, and their rise synchronises with the origin of the great houses of the Italian and Jewish bankers. Yet there was very little in the past learning of Christian teachers to guide them in these matters, for the patristic theories, which we have already described, and a few isolated passages cited in the Decretals of Gratian, formed as yet almost the only contribution to the study of these sciences. However, this absence of any organised body of knowledge was for them but one more stimulus towards the elaboration of a thorough synthesis of the moral aspect of wealth. A few of the earlier masters made reference, detached and personal, to the subject of dispute, but it was rather in the form of a disorderly comment than the definite statement of a theory.

Then came the translation of Aristotle's Politics, with the keen criticism they contain of the views Plato had advocated. Here at once the intellect of Europe found an exact exposition of principles, and began immediately to debate their excellence and their defect. St. Thomas Aquinas set to work on a literal commentary, and at his express desire an accurate translation was made direct from the Greek by his fellow-Dominican, William of Moerbeke. Later on, when all this had had time to settle and find its place, St. Thomas worked out his own theory of private property in two short articles in his famous Summa Theologica. In his treatise on Justice, which occupies a large proportion of the Secund Secundae of the Summa, he found himself forced to discuss the moral evil of theft; and to do this adequately he had first to explain what he meant by private possessions. Without these, of course, there could be no theft at all.

He began, therefore, by a preliminary article on the actual state of created things--that is, the material, so to say, out of which private property is evolved. Here he notes that the nature of things, their constituent essence, is in the hands of God, not man. The worker can change the form, and, in consequence, the value of a thing, but the substance which lies beneath all the outward show is too subtle for him to affect it in any way. To the Supreme Being alone can belong the power of creation, annihilation, and absolute mutation. But besides this tremendous force which God holds incommunicably, there is another which He has given to man, namely, the use of created things. For when man was made, he was endowed with the lordship of the earth. This lordship is obviously one without which he could not live. The air, and the forces of nature, the beasts of the field, the birds and fishes, the vegetation in fruit and root, and the stretches of corn are necessary for man's continued existence on the earth. Over them, therefore, he has this limited dominion.

Moreover, St. Thomas goes on, man has not merely the present moment to consider. He is a being possessed of intelligence and will, powers which demand and necessitate their own constant activity. Instinct, the gift of brute creation, ensures the preservation of life by its blind preparation for the morrow. Man has no such ready-made and spontaneous faculty. His powers depend for their effectiveness on their deliberative and strenuous exertions. And because life is a sacred thing, a lamp of which the once extinguished light cannot be here re-enkindled, it carries with it, when it is intelligent and volitional, the duty of self-preservation. Accordingly the human animal is bound by the law of his own being to provide against the necessities of the future. He has, therefore, the right to acquire not merely what will suffice for the instant, but to look forward and arrange against the time when his power of work shall have lessened, or the objects which suffice for his personal needs become scarcer or more difficult of attainment. Property, therefore, of some kind or other, says Aquinas, is required by the very nature of man. Individual possessions are not a mere adventitious luxury which time has accustomed him to imagine as something he can hardly do without, nor are they the result of civilised culture, which by the law of its own development creates fresh needs for each fresh demand supplied; but in some form or other they are an absolute and dire necessity, without which life could not be lived at all. Not simply for his "well-being," but for his very existence, man finds them to be a sacred need. Thus as they follow directly from the nature of creation, we can term them "natural."

St. Thomas then proceeds in his second article
to enter into the question of the rights of
private property. The logical result of his
previous argument is only to affirm the need
man has of some property; the practice of
actually dividing goods among individuals
requires further elaboration if it is to be
reasonably defended. Man must have the use of
the fruits of the earth, but why these rather than
those should belong to him is an entirely
different problem. It is the problem of
Socialism. For every socialist must demand for
each member of the human race the right to
some possessions, food and other such
necessities. But why he should have this
particular thing, and why that other thing
should belong to someone else, is the question
which lies at the basis of all attempts to preserve
or destroy the present fabric of society. Now,
the argument which we have so far cited from
St. Thomas is simply based on the indefeasible
right of the individual to the maintenance of his
life. Personality implies the right of the
individual to whatever is needful to him in
achieving his earthly purpose, but does not in
itself justify the right to private property.

"Two offices pertain to man with regard to exterior things" (thus he continues). "The first is the power of procuring and dispensing, and in respect to this, it is lawful for man to hold things as his own." Here it is well to note that St. Thomas in this single sentence teaches that private property, or the individual occupation of actual land or capital or instruments of wealth, is not contrary to the moral law. Consequently he would repudiate the famous epigram, "La Propriété c'est le vol." Man may hold and dispose of what belongs to him, may have private property, and in no way offend against the principles of justice, whether natural or divine.

But in the rest of the article St. Thomas goes farther still. Not merely does he hold the moral proposition that private property is lawful, but he adds to it the social proposition that private property is necessary. "It is even necessary," says he, "for human life, and that for three reasons. Firstly, because everyone is more solicitous about procuring what belongs to himself alone than that which is common to all or many, since each shunning labour leaves to another what is the common burden of all, as happens with a multitude of servants. Secondly, because human affairs are conducted in a more orderly fashion if each has his own duty of procuring a certain thing, while there would be confusion if each should procure things haphazard. Thirdly, because in this way the peace of men is better preserved, for each is content with his own. Whence we see that strife more frequently arises among those who hold a thing in common and individually. The other office which is man's concerning exterior things, is the use of them; and with regard to this a man ought not to hold exterior things as his own, but as common to all, that he may portion them out to others readily in time of need." (The translation is taken from New Things and Old, by H. C. O'Neill, 1909, London, pp. 253-4.) The wording and argument of this will bear, and is well worth, careful analysis. For St. Thomas was a man, as Huxley witnesses, of unique intellectual power, and, moreover, his theories on private property were immediately accepted by all the schoolmen. Each succeeding writer did little else than make more clear and defined the outlines of the reasoning here elaborated. We shall, therefore, make no further apology for an attempt to set out the lines of thought sketched by Aquinas.

It will be noticed at once that the principles on which private property are here based are of an entirely different nature from those by which the need of property itself was defended. For the latter we were led back to the very nature of man himself and confronted with his right and duty to preserve his own life. From this necessity of procuring supply against the needs of the morrow, and the needs of the actual hour, was deduced immediately the conclusion that property of some kind (i.e. the possession of some material things) was demanded by the law of man's nature. It was intended as an absolute justification of a sacred right. But in this second article a completely different process is observed. We are no longer considering man's essential nature in the abstract, but are becoming involved in arguments of concrete experience. The first was declared to be a sacred right, as it followed from a law of nature; the second is merely conditioned by the reasons brought forward to support it. To repeat the whole problem as it is put in the Summa, we can epitomise the reasoning of St. Thomas in this easier way. The question of property implies two main propositions: (a) the right to property, i.e. to the use of material creation; (b) the right to private property, i.e. to the actual division of material things among the determined individuals of a social group. The former is a sacred, inalienable right, which can never be destroyed, for it springs from the roots of man's nature. If man exists, and is responsible for his existence, then he must necessarily have the right to the means without which his existence is made impossible. But the second proposition must be determined quite differently. The kind of property here spoken of is simply a matter not of right, but of experienced necessity, and is to be argued for on the distinct grounds that without it worse things would follow: "it is even necessary for human life, and that for three reasons." This is a purely conditional necessity, and depends entirely on the practical effect of the three reasons cited. Were a state of society to exist in which the three reasons could no longer be urged seriously, then the necessity which they occasioned would also cease to hold. In point of fact, St. Thomas was perfectly familiar with a social group in which these conditions did not exist, and the law of individual possession did not therefore hold, namely, the religious orders. As a Dominican, he had defended his own

Order against the attacks of those who would have suppressed it altogether; and in his reply to William of St. Amour he had been driven to uphold the right to common life, and consequently to deny that private property was inalienable.

Of course it was perfectly obvious that for St. Thomas himself the idea of the Commune or the State owning all the land and capital, and allowing to the individual citizens simply the use of these common commodities, was no doubt impracticable; and the three reasons which he gives are his sincere justification of the need of individual ownership. Without this division of property, he considered that national life would become even more full of contention than it was already. Accordingly, it was for its effectiveness in preventing a great number of quarrels that he defended the individual ownership of property.

Besides this article, there are many other expressions and broken phrases in which Aquinas uses the same phrase, asserting that the actual division of property was due to human nature. "Each field considered in itself cannot be looked upon as naturally belonging to one rather than to another" (2, 2, 57, 3); "distinction of property is not inculcated by nature" (1a, 2ae, 94, 5); but again he is equally clear in insisting on the other proposition, that there is no moral law which forbids the possession of land in severalty. "The common claim upon things is traceable to the natural law, not because the natural law dictates that all things should be held in common, and nothing as belonging to any individual person, but because according to the natural law there is no distinction of possessions which comes by human convention" (2a, 2ae, 66, 2ad 1m.).

To apprehend the full significance of this last remark, reference must be made to the theories of the Roman legal writers, which have been already explained. The law of nature was looked upon as some primitive determination of universal acceptance, and of venerable sanction, which sprang from the roots of man's being. This in its absolute form could never be altered or changed; but there was besides another law which had no such compelling power, but which rested simply on the experience of the human race. This was reversible, for it depended on specific conditions and stages of development. Thus nature dictated no division of property, though it implied the necessity of some property; the need of the division was only discovered when men set to work to live in social intercourse. Then it was found that unless divisions were made, existence was intolerable; and so by human convention, as St. Thomas sometimes says, or by the law of nature, as he elsewhere expresses it, the division into private property was agreed upon and took place.

This elaborate statement of St. Thomas was widely accepted through all the Middle Ages. Wycliff alone, and a few like him, ventured to oppose it; but otherwise this extremely logical and moderate defence of existing institutions received general adhesion. Even Scotus, like Ockham, a brilliant Oxford scholar whose hidden tomb at Cologne finds such few pilgrims kneeling in its shade, so hardy in his thought and so eager to find a flaw in the arguments of Aquinas, has no alternative to offer. Franciscan though he was, and therefore, perhaps, more likely to favour communistic teaching, his own theory is but a repetition of what his rival had already propounded. Thus, for example, he writes in a typical passage: "Even supposing it as a principle of positive law that 'life must be lived peaceably in a state of polity,' it does not straightway follow 'Therefore everyone must have separate possessions.' For peace could be observed even if all things were in common. Nor even if we presuppose the wickedness of those who live together is it a necessary consequence. Still a distinction of property is decidedly in accord with a peaceful social life. For the wicked rather take care of their private possessions, and rather seek to appropriate to themselves than to the community common goods. Whence come strife and contention. Hence we find it (division of property) admitted in almost every positive law. And although there is a fundamental principle from which all other laws and rights spring, still from that fundamental principle positive human laws do not follow absolutely or immediately. Rather it is as declarations or explanations in detail of that general principle that they come into being, and must be considered as evidently in accord with the universal law of nature." (Super Sententias Quaestiones, Bk. 4, Dist. 15, q. 2. Venice, 1580.)

Here again, then, are the same salient points we have already noticed in the Summa. There is the idea clearly insisted on that the division of property is not a first principle nor an immediate deduction from a first principle, that in itself it is not dictated by the natural law which leaves all things in common, that it is, however, not contrary to natural law, but evidently in accord with it, that its necessity and its introduction were due entirely to the actual experience of the race.

Again, to follow the theory chronologically still farther forward, St. Antonino, whose charitable institutions in Florence have stamped deeply with his personality that scene of his life's labours, does little more than repeat the words of St. Thomas, though the actual phrase in which he here compresses many pages of argument is reproduced from a work by the famous Franciscan moralist John de Ripa. "It is by no means right that here upon earth fallen humanity should have all things in common, for the world would be turned into a desert, the way to fraud and all manner of evils would be opened, and the good would have always the worse, and the bad always the better, and the most effective means of destroying all peace would be established" (Summa Moralis, 3, 3, 2, 1). Hence he concludes that "such a community of goods never could benefit the State." These are none other arguments than those already advanced by St. Thomas. His articles, already quoted, are indeed the Locus Classicus for all mediaeval theorists, and, though references in every mediaeval work on social and economic questions are freely made to Aristotle's Politics, it is evident that it is really Aquinas who is intended.

Distinction of property, therefore, though declared so necessary for peaceable social life, does not, for these thinkers, rest on natural law, nor a divine law, but on positive human law under the guidance of prudence and authority. Communism is not something evil, but rather an ideal too lofty to be ever here realised. It implied so much generosity, and such a vigour of public spirit, as to be utterly beyond the reach of fallen nature. The Apostles alone could venture to live so high a life, "for their state transcended that of every other mode of living" (Ptolomeo of Lucca, De Regimine Principio, book iv., cap. 4, Parma, 1864, p. 273). However, that form of communism which entailed an absolutely even division of all wealth among all members of the group, though it had come to them on the authority of Phileas and Lycurgus, was indeed to be reprobated, for it contradicted the prime feature of all creation. God made all things in their proper number, weight, and measure. Yet in spite of all this it must be insisted on at the risk of repetition that the socialist theory of State ownership is never considered unjust, never in itself contrary to the moral law. Albertus Magnus, the master of Aquinas, and the leader in commenting on Aristotle's Politics, freely asserts that community of goods "is not impossible, especially among those who are well disciplined by the virtue of philanthropy--that is, the common love of all; for love, of its own nature, is generous." But to arrange it, the power of the State must be called into play; it cannot rest on any private authority. "This is the proper task of the legislator, for it is the duty of the legislator to arrange everything for the best advantage of the citizens" (In Politicis, ii. 2, p. 70, Lyons, 1651). Such, too, is the teaching of St. Antonino, who even goes so far as to assert that "just as the division of property at the beginning of historic time was made by the authority of the State, it is evident that the same authority is equally competent to reverse its decision and return to its earlier social organisation" (Summa Moralis, ii. 3, 2, Verona, 1740, p. 182). He lays down, indeed, a principle so broad that it is difficult to understand where it could well end: "That can be justly determined by the prince which is necessary for the peaceful intercourse of the citizens." And in defence he points triumphantly to the fact that the prince can set aside a just claim to property, and transfer it to another who happens to hold it by prescription, on the ground of the numerous disputes which might otherwise be occasioned. That is to say, that the law of his time already admitted that in certain circumstances the State could take what belonged to one and give it to another, without there being any fault on the part of the previous owner to justify its forfeiture; and he defends this proceeding on the axiom just cited (ibid., pp. 182-3), namely, its necessity "for the peaceful intercourse of the citizens."

The Schoolmen can therefore be regarded as a consistent and logical school. They had an extreme dislike to any broad generalisation, and preferred rather, whenever the occasion could be discovered, to distinguish rather than to concede or deny. Hence, confronted by the communistic theory of State ownership which had been advanced by Plato, and by a curious group of strange, heterodox teachers, and which had, moreover, the actual support of many patristic sayings, and the strong bias of monastic life, they set out joyfully to resolve it into the simplest and most unassailable series of propositions. They began, therefore, by admitting that nature made no division of property, and in that sense held all things in common; that in the early stages of human history, when man, as yet unfallen, was conceived as living in the Garden of Eden in perfect innocency, common property amply satisfied his sinless and unselfish moral character; that by the Fall lust and greed overthrew this idyllic state, and led to a continued condition of internecine strife, and the supremacy of might; that experience gradually brought men to realise that their only hope towards peaceful intercourse lay in the actual division of property, and the establishment of a system of private ownership; that this could only be set aside by men who were themselves perfect, or had vowed themselves to pursue perfection, namely, Our Lord, His Apostles, and the members of religious orders. To this list of what they held to be historic events they added another which contained the moral deductions to be made from these facts. This began by the assertion that private property in itself was not in any sense contrary to the virtue of justice; that it was entirely lawful; that it was even necessary on account of certain evil conditions which otherwise would prevail; that the State, however, had the right in extreme cases and for a just cause to transfer private property from one to another; that it could, when the needs of its citizens so demanded, reverse its primitive decision, and re-establish its earlier form of common ownership; that this last system, however possible, and however much it might be regretted as a vanished and lost ideal, was decidedly now a violent and impracticable proceeding.

These theories, it is evident, though they furnish the only arguments which are still in use among us to support the present social organisation, are also patent of an interpretation which might equally lead to the very opposite conclusion. In his fear of any general contradiction to communism which should be open to dispute, and in his ever-constant memory of his own religious life as a Dominican friar, Aquinas had to mark with precision to what extent and in what sense private property could be justified. But at the same time he was forced by the honesty of his logical training to concede what he could in favour of the other side. He took up in this question, as in every other, a middle course, in which neither extreme was admitted, but both declared to contain an element of truth. It is clear, too, that his scholastic followers, even to our own date, in their elaborate commentaries can find no escape from the relentless logic of his conclusions. Down the channel that he dug flowed the whole torrent of mediaeval and modern scholasticism.[2] But for those whose minds were practical rather than abstract, one or other proposition he advanced, isolated from the context of his thought, could be quoted as of moment, and backed by the greatness of his name. His assertion of the absolute impracticable nature of socialistic organisation, as he knew it in his own age, was too good a weapon to be neglected by those who sought about for means of defence for their own individualistic theories; whereas others, like the friars of whom Wycliff and Langland spoke, and who headed bands of luckless peasants in the revolt of 1381 against the oppression of an over-legalised feudalism, were blind to this remarkable expression of Aquinas' opinion, and quoted him only when he declared that "by nature all things were in common," and when he protested that the socialist theory of itself contained nothing contrary to the teaching of the gospel or the doctrines of the Church.

Truth is blinding in its brilliance. Half-truths are easy to see, and still easier to explain. Hence the full and detailed theory elaborated by the Schoolmen has been tortured to fit first one and then another scheme of political reform. Yet all the while its perfect adjustment of every step in the argument remains a wonderful monument of the intellectual delicacy and hardihood of the Schoolmen.

FOOTNOTE:

[2] Cf. Coutenson, Theologia Mentis et Cordis, iii. 388-389, Paris, 1875; and Billnart, De Justitia, i. 123-124, Liège, 1746.

CHAPTER V
THE LAWYERS

Besides the Schoolmen, by whom the problems of life were viewed in the refracted light of theology and philosophy, there was another important class in mediaeval times which exercised itself over the same social questions, but visaged them from an entirely different angle. This was the great brotherhood of the law, which, whether as civil or canonical, had its own theories of the rights of private ownership. It must be remembered, too, that just as the theologians supported their views by an appeal to what were considered historic facts in the origin of property, so, too, the legalists depended for the material of their judgment on circumstances which the common opinion of the time admitted as authentic.

When the West drifted out from the clouds of barbaric invasion, and had come into calm waters, society was found to be organised on a basis of what has been called feudalism. That is to say, the natural and universal result of an era of conquest by a wandering people is that the new settlers hold their possessions from the conqueror on terms essentially contractual. The actual agreements have varied constantly in detail, but the main principle has always been one of reciprocal rights and duties. So at the early dawn of the Middle Ages, after the period picturesquely styled the Wanderings of the Nations, we find the subjugating races have encamped in Europe, and hold it by a series of fiefs. The action, for example, of William the Norman, as plainly shown in Domesday Book, is typical of what had for some three or four centuries been happening here and on the Continent. Large tracts of land were parcelled out among the invading host, and handed over to individual barons to hold from the King on definite terms of furnishing him with men in times of war, of administering justice within their domains, and of assisting at his Council Board when he should stand in need of their advice. The barons, to suit their own convenience, divided up these territories among their own retainers on terms similar to those by which they held their own. And thus the whole organisation of the country was graduated from the King through the greater barons to tenants who held their possessions, whether a castle, or a farm, or a single hut, from another to whom they owed suit and service.

This roughly (constantly varying, and never actually quite so absolutely carried out) is the leading principle of feudalism. It is clearly based upon a contract between each man and his immediate lord; but, and this is of importance in the consideration of the feudal theory of private property, whatever rights and duties held good were not public, but private. There was not at the first, and in the days of what we may call "pure feudalism," any concept of a national law or natural right, but only a bundle of individual rights. Appeal from injustice was not made at a supreme law-court, but only to the courts of the barons to whom both litigants owed allegiance. The action of the King was quite naturally always directed towards breaking open this enclosed sphere of influence, and endeavouring to multiply the occasions on which his officials might interfere in the courts of his subjects. Thus the idea gradually grew up (and its growth is perhaps the most important matter of remark in mediaeval history), by which the King's law and the King's rights were looked upon as dominating those of individuals or groups. The courts baron and customary, and the sokes of privileged townships were steadily emptied of their more serious cases, and shorn of their primitive powers. This, too, was undoubtedly the reason for the royal interference in the courts Christian (the feudal name for the clerical criminal court). The King looked on the Church, as he looked on his barons and his exempted townships, as outside his royal supremacy, and, in consequence, quarrelled over investiture and criminous clerks, and every other point in which he had not as yet secured that his writs and judgments should prevail. There was a whole series of courts of law which were absolutely independent of his officers and his decision. His restless energy throughout this period had, therefore, no other aim than to bring all these into a line with his own, and either to capture them for himself, or to reduce them to sheer impotence. But at the beginning there was little notion of a royal judge who should have power to determine cases in which barons not immediately holding their fiefs of the King were implicated. The concern of each was only with the lord next above him. And the whole conception of legal rights was, therefore, considered simply as private rights.

The growth of royal power consequently acted most curiously on contemporary thinkers. It meant centralisation, the setting up of a definite force which should control the whole kingdom. It resulted in absolutism increasing, with an ever-widening sphere of royal control. It culminated in the Reformation, which added religion to the other departments of State in which royal interference held predominance. Till then the Papacy, as in some sort "a foreign power," world-wide and many-weaponed, could treat on more than equal terms with any European monarch, and secure independence for the clergy. With the lopping off of the national churches from the parent stem, this energising force from a distant centre of life ceased. Each separate clerical organisation could now depend only on its own intrinsic efficiency. For most this meant absolute surrender.

The civil law therefore which supplanted feudalism entailed two seemingly contradicting principles which are of importance in considering the ownership of land. On the one hand, the supremacy of the King was assured. The people became more and more heavily taxed, their lands were subjected to closer inspection, their criminal actions were viewed less as offences against individuals than as against the peace of the King. It is an era in which, therefore, as we have already stated, the power of the individual sinks gradually more and more into insignificance in comparison with the rising force of the King's dominion. Private rights are superseded by public rights.

Yet, on the other hand, and by the development of identically the same principles, the individual gains. His tenure of land becomes far less a matter of contract. He himself escapes from his feudal chief, and his inferior tenants slip also from his control. He is no longer one in a pyramid of grouped social organisation, but stands now as an individual answerable only to the head of the State. He has duties still; but no longer a personal relationship to his lord. It is the King and that vague abstraction called the State which now claim him as a subject; and by so doing are obliged to recognise his individual status. This new and startling prominence of the individual disturbed the whole concept of ownership. Originally under the influence of that pure feudalism which nowhere existed in its absolute form, the two great forces in the life of each member of the social group were his own and that of his immediate lord. These fitted together into an almost indissoluble union; and therefore absolute ownership of the soil was theoretically impossible. Now, however, the individual was emancipated from his lord. He was still, it is true, subject to the King, whose power might be a great deal more oppressive than the barons' had been. But the King was far off, whereas the baron had been near, and nearly always in full evidence. Hence the result was the emphasis of the individual's absolute dominion. Not, indeed, as though it excluded the dominion of the King, but precisely because the royal predominance could only be recognised by the effective shutting out of the interference of the lord. To exclude the "middle-man," the King was driven to recognise the absolute dominion of the individual over his own possessions.

This is brought out in English law by Bracton and his school. Favourers as they were of the royal prerogative, they were driven to take up the paradoxical ground that the King was not the sole owner of property. To defend the King they were obliged to dispossess him. To put his control on its most effective basis, they had no other alternative left them than to admit the fullest rights of the individual against the King. For only if the individual had complete ownership, could there be no interference on the part of the lord; only if the possessions of the tenants were his own, were they prevented from falling under the baronial jurisdiction. Therefore by apparently denying the royal prerogative the civil lawyers were in effect, as they perfectly well recognised, really extending it and enabling it to find its way into cases and courts where it could not else well have entered.

Seemingly, therefore, all idea of socialism or nationalisation of land (at that date the great means of production) was now excluded. The individualistic theory of property had suddenly appeared; and simultaneously the old group forms, which implied collectivism in some shape or other, ceased any longer to be recognised as systems of tenure. Yet, at the same time, by a paradox as evident as that by which the civilians exalted the royal prerogative apparently at its own expense, or as that by which Wycliff's communism is found to be in reality a justification of the policy of leaving things as they are, while St. Thomas's theory of property is discovered as far less oppressive and more adaptable to progressive developments of national wealth, it is noticed that, from the point of view of the socialist, monarchical absolutism is the most favourable form of a State's constitution. For wherever a very strictly centralised system of government exists, it is clear that a machinery, which needs little to turn it to the advantage of the absolute rule of a rebellious minority, has been already constructed. In a country where, on the other hand, local government has been enormously encouraged, it is obviously far more difficult for socialism to force an entrance into each little group. There are all sorts of local conditions to be squared, vagaries of law and administration to be reduced to order, connecting bridges to be thrown from one portion of the nation to the next, so as to form of it one single whole. Were the socialists of to-day to seize on the machinery of government in Germany and Russia, they could attain their purposes easily and smoothly, and little difference in constitutional forms would be observed in these countries, for already the theory of State ownership and State interference actually obtains. They would only have to substitute a bloc for a man. But in France and England, where the centralisation is far less complete, the success of the socialistic party and its achievement of supreme power would mean an almost entire subversal of all established methods of administration, for all the threads would have first to be gathered into a single hand.

Consequently feudalism, which turned the landowners into petty sovereigns and insisted on local courts, &c., though seemingly communistic or socialistic, was really, from its intense local colouring, far less easy of capture by those who favoured State interference. It was individualistic, based on private rights. But the new royal prerogative led the way to the consideration of the evident ease by which, once the machine was possessed, the rest of the system could without difficulty be brought into harmony with the new theories. To make use of comparison, it was Cardinal Wolsey's assumption of full legatine power by permission of the Pope which first suggested to Henry VIII that he could dispense with His Holiness altogether. He saw that the Cardinal wielded both spiritual and temporal jurisdiction. He coveted his minister's position, and eventually achieved it by ousting both Clement and Wolsey, who had unwittingly shown him in which way more power lay.

So, similarly, the royal despotism itself, by centralising all power into the hands of a single prince, accustomed men to the idea of the absolute supremacy of national law, drove out of the field every defender of the rights of minorities, and thus paved the way for the substitution of the people for itself. The French Revolution was the logical conclusion to be drawn from the theories of Louis XIV. It needed only the fire of Rousseau to burn out the adventitious ornamentation which in the shape of that monarch's personal glorification still prevented the naked structure from being seen in all its clearness. L'Etat c'est moi can be as aptly the watchword of a despotic oligarchy, or a levelling socialism, as of a kingly tyranny, according as it passes from the lips of the one to the few or the many. It is true that the last phase was not completed till long after the Middle Ages had closed, but the tendency towards it is evident in the teachings of the civil lawyers.

Thus, for example, State absolutism is visible in the various suggestions made by men like Pierre du Bois and Wycliff (who, in the expression of their thoughts, are both rather lawyers than schoolmen) to dispossess the clergy of their temporalities. The principles urged, for instance, by these two in justification of this spoliation could be applied equally well to the estates of laymen. For the same principles put into the King's hand the undetermined power of doing what was necessary for the well-being of the State. It is true that Pierre du Bois (De Recuperatione Terre Sancte, pp. 39-41, 115-8) asserted that the royal authority was limited to deal in this way with Church lands, and could not touch what belonged to others. But this proviso was obviously inserted so arbitrarily that its logical force could not have had any effect. Political necessity alone prevented it from being used against the nobility and gentry.

Ockham, however, the clever Oxford Franciscan, who formed one of the group of pamphleteers that defended Louis of Bavaria against Pope John XXII, quite clearly enlarged the grounds for Church disendowment so as to include the taking over by the State of all individual property. He was a thinker whose theories were strangely compounded of absolutism and democracy. The Emperor was to be supported because his autocracy came from the people. Hence, when Ockham is arguing about ecclesiastical wealth, and the way in which it could be quite fairly confiscated by the Government, he enters into a discussion about the origin of the imperial dignity. This, he declares, was deliberately handed over by the people to the Emperor. To escape making the Pope the original donor of the imperial title, Ockham concedes that privilege to the people. It was they, the people, who had handed over to the Caesars of the Holy Roman Empire all their own rights and powers. Hence Louis was a monarch whose absolutism rested on a popular basis. Then he proceeds in his argument to say that the human positive law by which private property was introduced was made by the people themselves, and that the right or power by which this was done was transferred by them to the Emperor along with the imperial dignity.

Louis, therefore, had the same right to undo what they had done, for in him all their powers now resided. This, of course, formed an excellent principle from which to argue to his right to dispossess the Church of its superfluous wealth--indeed of all its wealth. But it could prove equally effectual against the holding by the individual of any property whatever. It made, in effect, private ownership rest on the will of the prince.

Curiously, too, in quite another direction the same form of argument had been already worked out by Nicole Oresme, a famous Bishop of Lisieux, who first translated into French the Politics of Aristotle, and who helped so largely in the reforms of Charles V of France. His great work was in connection with the revision of the coinage, on which he composed a celebrated treatise. He held that the change of the value of money, either by its deliberate depreciation, or by its being brought back to its earlier standard of face value, carried such widespread consequences that the people should most certainly be consulted on it. It was not fair to them to take such a step without their willing co-operation. Yet he admits fully that, though this is the wiser and juster way of acting, there was no absolute need for so doing, since all possession and all property sprang from the King. And this last conclusion was advocated by his rival, Philip de Meziers, whose advice Charles ultimately followed. Philip taught that the king was sole judge of whatever was for public use.

But there was a further point in the same question which afforded matter for an interesting discussion among the lawyers. Pope

Innocent IV, who had first been famous as a
canonist, and retained as Pontiff his old love for
disputations of this kind, developed a theory of
his own on the relation between the right of the
individual to possess and the right of the State
over that possession. He distinguished carefully
between two entirely different concepts,
namely, the right and its exercise. The first he
admitted to be sacred and inviolable, because it
sprang from the very nature of man. It could
not be disturbed or in any way molested; the
State had therefore no power to interfere with
the right. But he suggested that the exercise of
that right, or, to use his actual phrase, the
"actions in accord with that right," rested on the
basis of civil, positive law, and could therefore
be controlled by legal decisions. The right was
sacred, its exercise was purely conventional.
Thus every man has a right to property; he can
never by any possible means divest himself of it,
for it is rooted in the depths of his being, and
supported by his human nature. But this right
appears especially to be something internal,
intrinsic. For him to exercise it--that is to say, to
hold this land or that, or indeed any land at all--
the State's intervention must be secured. At
least the State can control his action in buying,

selling, or otherwise obtaining it. His right cannot be denied, but for reasons of social importance its exercise well may be. Nor did this then appear as a merely unmeaning distinction; he would not admit that a right which could not be exercised was hardly worth consideration. And, in point of fact, the Pope's private theory found very many supporters.

There were others, however, who judged it altogether too fantastical. The most interesting of his opponents was a certain Antonio Roselli, a very judiciously-minded civil lawyer, who goes very thoroughly into the point at issue. He gives Innocent's views, and quotes what authority he can find for them in the Digest and Decretals. But for himself he would prefer to admit that the right to private property is not at all sacred or natural in the sense of being inviolable. He willingly concedes to the State the right to judge all claims of possession. This is the more startling since ordinarily his views are extremely moderate, and throughout the controversy between Pope and Emperor he succeeded in steering a very careful, delicate course. To him, however, all rights to property were purely civil and arguable only on principles of positive law. There was no need, therefore, to discriminate between the right and its exercise, for both equally could be controlled by the State. There are evidences to show that he admitted the right of each man to the support of his own life, and, therefore, to private property in the form of actual food, &c., necessary for the immediate moment; but he distinctly asserts as his own personal idea that "the prince could take away my right to a thing, and any exercise of that right," adding only that for this there must be some cause. The prince cannot arbitrarily confiscate property; he must have some reasonable motive of sufficient gravity to outweigh the social inconveniences which confiscation would necessarily produce. Not every cause is a sufficient one, but those only which concern "public liberty or utility." Hence he decides that the Pope cannot alienate Church lands without some justifying reason, nor hand them over to the prince unless there happens to be an urgent need, springing from national circumstances. It does not follow, however, that he wishes to make over to the State absolute right to individual property under normal conditions. The individual has the sole dominion over his own possessions; that dominion reverts to the State only in some

extreme instance. His treatise, therefore
(Goldast, De Monarchia, 1611-1614, Hanover,
p. 462, &c.), may be looked upon as summing
up the controversy as it then stood. The legal
distinction suggested by Innocent IV had been
given up by the lawyers as insufficient. The
theories of Du Bois, Wycliff, Ockham, and the
others had ceased to have much significance,
because they gave the royal power far too
absolute a jurisdiction over the possessions of
its subjects. The feudal contractual system,
which these suggested reforms had intended to
drive out, had failed for entirely different
reasons, and could evidently be brought back
only at the price of a complete and probably
unsuccessful disturbance of the social and
economic organisation. The centralisation
which had risen on the ruins of the older local
sovereignties and immunities, had brought with
it an emphasised recognition of the public rights
and duties of all subjects, and had at the same
time confirmed the individual in the ownership
of his little property, and given him at the last
not a conditional, but an absolute possession.
To safeguard this, and to prevent it from
becoming a block in public life, a factor of
discontent, the lawyers were engaged in framing

an additional clause which should give to the State an ultimate jurisdiction, and would enable it to overrule any objections on the part of the individual to a national policy or law. The suggested distinction that the word "right" should be emptied of its deeper meaning, by refusing it the further significance of "exercise," was too subtle and too legal to obtain much public support. So that the lawyers were driven to admit that for a just cause the very right itself could be set aside, and every private possession (when public utility and liberty demanded it) confiscated or transferred to another.

Even the right to compensation for such confiscation was with equal cleverness explained away. For it was held that, when an individual had lost his property through State action, and without his having done anything to deserve it as a punishment, compensation could be claimed. But whenever a whole people or nation was dispossessed by the State, there was no such right at all to any indemnity.

Thus was the wholesale adoption of land-nationalism to be justified. Thus could the State capture all private possessions without any fear of being guilty of robbery. It was considered that it was only the oppression of the individual and class spoliation which really contravened the moral law.

The legal theories, therefore, which supplanted the old feudal concepts were based on the extension of royal authority, and the establishment of public rights. Individualistic possession was emphasised; yet the simultaneous setting up of the absolute monarchies of the sixteenth century really made their ultimate capture by the Socialist party more possible.

CHAPTER VI
THE SOCIAL REFORMERS

It may seem strange to class social reforms under the wider heading of Socialistic Theories, and the only justification for doing so is that which we have already put forward in defence of the whole book; namely, that the term "socialistic" has come to bear so broad an interpretation as to include a great deal that does not strictly belong to it. And it is only on the ground of their advocating State interference in the furtherance of their reforms that the reformers here mentioned can be spoken of as socialistic.

Of course there have been reformers in every age who came to bring to society their own personal measures of relief. But in the Middle Ages hardly a writer took pen in hand who did not note in the body politic some illness, and suggest some remedy. Howsoever abstruse might be the subject of the volume, there was almost sure to be a reference to economic or social life. It was not an epoch of specialists such as is ours. Each author composed treatises in almost every branch of learning. The same professor, according to mediaeval notions, might lecture to-day on Scripture, to-morrow on theology or philosophy, and the day after on natural science. For them a university was a place where each student learnt, and each professor taught, universal knowledge. Still from time to time men came to the front with some definite social message to be delivered to their own generation. Some were poets like Langland, some strike-leaders like John Ball, some religious enthusiasts like John Wycliff, some royal officials like Pierre du Bois.

This latter in his famous work addressed to
King Edward I of England (De Recuperatione
Sancte Terre), has several most interesting and
refreshing chapters on the education of women.
His bias is always against religious orders, and,
consequently, he favours the suppression of
almost every conventual establishment. Still, as
these were at his own date the only places
where education could be considered to exist at
all, he had to elaborate for himself a plan for the
proper instruction of girls. First, of course, the
nunneries must be confiscated by Government.
For him this was no act of injustice, since he
regarded the possessions of the whole clerical
body as something outside the ordinary laws of
property. But having in this way cleared the
ground of all rivals, and captured some
magnificent buildings, he can now go forward
in his scheme of education. He insists on having
only lay-mistresses, and prescribes the course of
study which these are to teach. There should be,
he held, many lectures on literature, and music,
and poetry, and the arts and crafts of home life.
Embroidery and home-management are
necessities for the woman's work in after years,
so they must be acquired in these schools. But
education cannot limit itself to these branches

of useful knowledge. It must take the woman's intelligence and develop that as skilfully as it does the man's. She is not inferior to him in power of reason, but only in her want of its right cultivation. Hence the new schools are to train her to equal man in all the arts of peace. Such is the main point in his programme, which even now sounds too progressive for the majority of our educational critics. He appeals for State interference that the colleges may be endowed out of the revenues of the religious houses, and that they may be supported in such a fashion as would always keep them abreast of the growing science of the times. And when, after a schooling of such a kind as this, the girls go out into their life-work as wives and mothers, he would wish them a more complete equality with their men-folk than custom then allowed. The spirit of freedom which is felt working through all his papers makes him the apostle of what would now be called the "new woman."

After him, there comes a lull in reforming ideas. But half a century later occurs a very curious and sudden outburst of rebellion all over Europe. From about the middle of the fourteenth century to the early fifteenth there seemed to be an epidemic of severe social unrest. There were at Paris, which has always been the nursery of revolutions, four separate risings. Etienne Marcel, who, however, was rather a tribune of the people than a revolutionary leader, came into prominence in 1355; he was followed by the Jacquerie in 1358, by the Maillotins in 1382, and the Cabochiens in 1411. In Rome we know of Rienzi in 1347, who eventually became hardly more than a popular demagogue; in Florence there was the outbreak of Ciompi in 1378; in Bohemia the excesses of Taborites in 1409; in England the Peasant Revolt of 1381.

It is perfectly obvious that a series of social disturbances of this nature could not leave the economic literature of the succeeding period quite as placid as it had found it. We notice now that, putting away questions of mere academic character, the thinkers and writers concern themselves with the actual state of the people. Parliament has its answer to the problem in a long list of statutes intended to muzzle the turbulent and restless revolutionaries. But this could not satisfy men who set their thought to study the lives and circumstances of their fellow-citizens. Consequently, as a result, we can notice the rise of a school of writers who interest themselves above all things in the economic conditions of labour. Of this school the easiest exponent to describe is Antonino of Florence, Archbishop and canonised saint. His four great volumes on the exposition of the moral law are fascinating as much for the quotations of other moralists which they contain, as for the actual theories of the saint himself. For the Archbishop cites on almost every page contemporary after contemporary who had had his say on the same problems. He openly asserts that he has read widely, taken notes of all his reading, has deliberately formed his opinions on the judgments, reasoned or merely expressed, of his authors. To read his books, then, is to realise that Antonino is summing up the whole experience of his generation. Indeed he was particularly well placed for one who wished for information. Florence, then at the height of its renown under the brilliant despotism of Cosimo dei Medici, was the scene where the great events of the life of Antonino took place. There he had seen within the city walls, three Popes, a Patriarch of Constantinople, the Emperors of East and West, and the most eminent men of both civilisations. He had taken part in a General Council of the Church, and knew thinkers as widely divergent as Giovanni Dominici and Æneas Sylvius Piccolomini. He was, therefore, more likely than most to have heard whatever theories were proposed by the various great political statesmen of Europe, whether they were churchmen or lawyers. Consequently, his schemes, as we might well expect, are startlingly advanced.

He begins by attacking the growing spirit of usury, and the resulting idleness. Men were finding out that under the new conditions which governed the money market it was possible to make a fortune without having done a day's work. The sons of the aristocracy of Florence, which was built up of merchant princes, and which had amassed its own fortunes in honest trading, had been tempted by the bankers to put their wealth out to interest, and to live on the surplus profit. The ease and security with which this could be done made it a popular investment, especially among the young men of fashion who came in, simply by inheritance, for large sums of money. As a consequence Florence found itself, for the first time in its history, beginning to possess a wealthy class of men who had never themselves engaged in any profession. The old reverence, therefore, which had always existed in the city for the man who laboured in his art or guild, began to slacken. No longer was there the same eagerness noticeable which used to boast openly that its rewards consisted in the consciousness of work well done. Instead, idleness became the badge of gentility, and trade a slur upon a man's reputation. No city can long survive so listless and languid an ideal. The Archbishop, therefore, denounced this new method of usurious traffic, and hinted further that to it was due the fierce rebellion which had for a while plunged Florence into the horrors of the Jacquerie. Wealth, he taught, should not of itself breed wealth, but only through the toil of honest labour, and that labour should be the labour of oneself, not of another.

Then he proceeded to argue that as upon the husband lies the labour of trade, the greater portion of his day must necessarily be passed outside the circle of family life. The breadwinner can attend neither to works of piety nor of charity in the way he should, and, consequently, to his wife it must be left to supply for his defects. She must take his place in the church, and amid the slums of the poor; she must for him and his lift her hands in prayer, and dispense his superfluous wealth in succouring the poverty-stricken. For the Archbishop will have none of the soothing doctrine which the millionaire preaches to the mob. He asserts that poverty is not a good thing; in itself it is an evil, and can be considered to lead only accidentally to any good. When, therefore, it assumes the form of destitution, every effort must be made to banish it from the State. For if it were to become at all prevalent in a nation, then would that people be on the pathway to its ruin. The politicians should therefore make it the end of their endeavours--though this, it may be, is an ideal which can never be fully brought to realisation-- to leave each man in a state of sufficiency. No one, for whatever reason, should be allowed to become destitute. Even should it be by his own fault that he were brought low, he must be provided for by the State, which has, however, in these circumstances, at the same time, the duty of punishing him.

But he remarks that the cause of poverty is more often the unjust rate of wages. The competition even of those days made men beat each other down in clamouring for work to be given them, and afforded to the employers an opportunity of taking workers who willingly accepted an inadequate scale of remuneration. This state of things he considered to be unjustifiable and unjust. No one had any right to make profit out of the wretchedness of the poor. Each human being had the duty of supporting his own life, and this he could not do except by the hiring of his own labour to another. That other, therefore, by the immutable laws of justice, when he used the powers of his fellow-man, was obliged in conscience to see that those powers could be fittingly sustained by the commodity which he exchanged for them. That is, the employer was bound to take note that his employees received such return for their labour as should compensate them for his use of it. The payment promised and given should be, in other words, what we would now speak of as a "living wage." But further, above this mere margin, additional rewards should be added according to the skill of the workman, or the dangerous nature of his employment, or the number of his children. The wages also should be paid promptly, without delay.

But it may sometimes happen that the labour which a man can contribute is not of such a kind as will enable him to receive the fair remuneration that should suffice for his bodily comfort. The saint is thinking of boy-labour, and the case of those too enfeebled by age or illness to work adequately, or perhaps at all. What is to be done for them? Let the State look to it, is his reply. The community must, by the law of its own existence, support all its members, and out of its superfluous wealth must provide for its weaker citizens. Those, therefore, who can labour harder than they need, or who already possess more riches than suffice for them, are obliged by the natural law of charity to give to those less favourably circumstanced than themselves.

St. Antonino does not, therefore, pretend to advocate any system of rigid equality among men. There is bound to be, in his opinion, variety among them, and from this variety comes indeed the harmony of the universe. For some are born to rule, and others, by the feebleness of their understanding or of their will, are fitted only to obey. The workman and servant must faithfully discharge the duties of their trade or service, be quick to receive a command, and reverent in their obedience. And the masters, in their turn, must be forbearing in their language, generous in their remuneration, and temperate in their commands. It is their business to study the powers of each of those whom they employ, and to measure out the work to each one according to the capacity which is discoverable in him. When a faithful labourer has become ill, the employer must himself tend and care for him, and be in no hurry to send him to a hospital.

About the hospitals themselves he has his own ideas, or at least he has picked out the sanest that he can find in the books and conversation of people whom he has come across. He insists strongly that women should, as matrons and nurses, manage those institutions which are solely for the benefit of women; and even in those where men also are received, he can see no incompatibility in their being administered by these same capable directors. He much commends the custom of chemists in Florence on Sundays, feast-days, and holidays of opening their dispensaries in turn. So that even should all the other shops be closed, there would always be one place open where medicines and drugs could be obtained in an emergency.

The education of the citizens, too, is another work which the State must consider. It is not something merely optional which is to be left to the judgment of the parent. The Archbishop holds that its proper organisation is the duty of the prince. Education, in his eyes, means that the children must be taught the knowledge of God, of letters, and of the arts and crafts they are to pursue in after life.

Again, he has thought out the theory of taxation. He admits its necessity. The State is obliged to perform certain duties for the community. It is obliged, for example, to make its roads fit for travelling, and so render them passable for the transfer of merchandise. It is bound to clear away all brigandage, highway robbery, and the like, for were this not done, no merchant would venture out through that State's territory, and its people would accordingly suffer.

Hence, again, he deduces the need for some sort of army, so that the goods of the citizens may be secured against the invader, for without this security there would be no stimulus to trade. Bridges must be built, and fords kept in repair. Since, therefore, the State is obliged to incur expenses in order to attain these objects, the State has the right, and indeed the duty, to order it so that the community shall pay for the benefits which it is to receive. Hence follows taxation.

But he sees at once that this power of demanding forced contributions from wealthy members of society needs safeguarding against abuse. Thus he is careful to insist that taxation can be valid only when it is levied by public authority, else it becomes sheer brigandage. No less is it to be reprobated when ordered indeed by public authority, but not used for public benefit. Thus, should it happen that a prince or other ruler of a State extorted money from his subjects on pretence of keeping the roads in good order, or similar works for the advantage of the community, and yet neglected to put the contributions of his people to this use, he would be defrauding the public, and guilty of treason against his country. So, too, to lay heavier burdens on his subjects than they could bear, or to graduate the scale in such a fashion as to weigh more heavily on one class than another, would be, in the ruler, an aggravated form of theft. Taxation must therefore be decreed by public authority, and be arranged according to some reasonable measure, and rest on the motive of benefiting the social organisation.

The citizens therefore who are elected to settle the incidence of taxation must be careful to take account of the income of each man, and so manage that on no one should the burden be too oppressive. He suggests himself the percentage of one pound per hundred. Nor, again, must there be any deliberate attempt to penalise political opponents, or to make use of taxation in order to avenge class-oppression. Were this to be done, the citizens so acting would be bound to make restitution to the persons whom they had thus injured.

Then St. Antonino takes the case of those who make a false declaration of their income. These, too, he convicts of injustice, and requires of them that they also should make restitution, but to the State. An exception to this, however, he allows. For if it happens to be the custom for each to make a declaration of income which is obviously below the real amount, then simply because all do it and all are known to do it, there is no obligation for the individual to act differently from his neighbours. It is not injustice, for the law evidently recognises the practice. And were he, on the other hand, to announce his full yearly wage of earnings, he would allow himself to be taxed beyond the proper measure of value. But to refuse to pay, or to elude by some subterfuge the just contribution which a man owes of his wealth to the easing of the public burdens, is in the eyes of the Archbishop a crime against the State. It would be an act of injustice, of theft, all the more heinous in that, as he declares with a flash of the energy of Rousseau, the "common good is something almost divine."

We have dwelt rather at length on the schemes of this one economist, and may seem, therefore, to have overlooked the writings of others equally full of interest. But the reason has been because this Florentine moralist does stand so perfectly for a whole school. He has read omnivorously, and has but selected most of his thoughts. He compares himself, indeed, in one passage of these volumes, to the laborious ant, "that tiny insect which wanders here and there, and gathers together what it thinks to be of use to its community." He represents a whole school, and represents it at its best, for there is no extreme dogmatism in him, no arguing from grounds that are purely arbitrary, or from a priori principles. It is his knowledge of the people among whom he had laboured so long which fits him to speak of the real sufferings of the poor. But experience requires for its being effectually put to the best advantage, that it should be wielded by one whose judgment is sober and careful. Now, St. Antonino was known in his own day as Antonino the Counsellor; and his justly-balanced decision, his delicately-poised advice, the straightness of his insight, are noticeable in the masterly way in which he sums up all the best that earlier and contemporary writers had devised in the domain of social economics.

There is, just at the close of the period with which this book deals, a rising school of reformers who can be grouped round More's Utopia. Some foreshadowed him, and others continued his speculations. Men like Harrington in his Oceana, and Milton in his Areopagitica, really belong to the same band; but life for them had changed very greatly, and already become something far more complex than the earlier writers had had to consider. There seemed no possibility of reforming it by the simple justice which St. Antonino and his fellows judged to be sufficient to set things back again as they had been in the Golden Age. The new writers are rather political than social. For them, as for the Greeks, it is the constitution which must be repaired. Whereas the mediaeval socialists thought, as St. Thomas indeed never wearied of repeating, that unrest and discontent would continue under any form of government whatever. The more each city changed its constitution, the more it remained the same. Florence, whether under a republic or a despotism, was equally happy and equally sad. For it was the spirit of government alone which, in the eyes of the scholastic social writers, made the State what it happened to be.

In this the modern sociologist of to-day finds himself more akin with the mediaeval thinkers than with the idealists of the parliamentary era in England, or of the Revolution in France. These fixed their hopes on definite organisations of government, and on the exact balance of executive and legislative powers. But for Scotus, and Wycliff, and St. Antonino, the cause of the evil is far deeper and more personal. Not in any form of the constitution, nor in any division of ruling authority, nor in its union under a firm despot, nor in the divine right of kings, or nobles, or people, was security to be found, or the well-ordering of the nation. But peace and rest from faction could be achieved with certainty only on the conditions of strict justice between man and man, on the observance of God's commandments.

Bede Jarrett, O.P., M.A.

CHAPTER VII
THE THEORY OF ALMSGIVING

Any description of mediaeval socialistic ideals which contained no reference to mediaeval notions of almsgiving would not be complete. Almsgiving was for them a necessary corollary to their theories of private possession. In the passage already quoted from St. Thomas Aquinas (p. 45), wherein he sets forth the theological aspect of property, he makes use of a broad distinction between what he calls "the power of procuring and dispensing" exterior things and "the use of them." We have already at some length tried to show what economists then meant by this first "power." Now we must establish the significance of what they intended by the second. And to do this the more clearly it will be as well to repeat the words in which St. Thomas briefly notes it: "The other office which is man's concerning exterior things is the use of them; and with regard to this a man ought not to hold exterior things as his own, but as common to all, that he may portion them out readily to others in time of need."

In this sentence is summed up the whole mediaeval concept of the law of almsdeeds.

Private property is allowed--is, in fact, necessary for human life--but on certain conditions. These imply that the possession of property belongs to the individual, but also that the use of it is not limited to him. The property is private, the use should be common. Indeed, it is only this common enjoyment which at all justifies private possession. It was as obvious then as now that there were inequalities in life, that one man was born to ease or wealth, or a great name, whereas another came into existence without any of these advantages, perhaps even hampered by positive disadvantages. Henry of Langenstein (1325-1397) in his famous Tractatus de Contractibus (published among the works of Gerson at Cologne, 1484, tom. iv. fol. 188), draws out this variety of fortune and misfortune in a very detailed fashion, and puts before his reader example after example of what they were then likely to have seen. But all the while he has his reason for so doing. He acknowledges the fact, and proceeds from it to build up his own explanation of it. The world is filled with all these men in their differing circumstances. Now, to make life possible for them, he asserts that private property is necessary. He is very energetic in his insistence upon that point.

Without private property he thinks that there
will be continual strife in which might, and not
right, will have the greater probability of
success. But simultaneously, and as a corrective
to the evils which private property of itself
would cause there should be added to it the
condition of common use. That is to say, that
although I own what is mine, yet I should put
no obstacle in the way of its reasonable use by
others. This is, of course, really the ideal of
Aristotle in his book of Politics, when he makes
his reply to Plato's communism. In Plato's
judgment, the republic should be governed in
the reverse way, Common property and private
use; he would really make this, which is a
feature of monastic life, compulsory on all. But
Aristotle, looking out on the world, an observer
of human nature, a student of the human heart,
sets up as more feasible, more practical, the
phrase which the Middle Ages repeat, Private
property and common use. The economics of a
religious house are hardly of such a kind,
thought the mediaevalists, as to suit the ways
and fancies of this workaday world.

But the Middle Ages do not simply repeat, they
Christianise Aristotle. They are dominated by
his categories of thought, but they perfect them

in the light of the New Dispensation. Faith is added to politics, love of the brotherhood is made to extend the mere brutality of the economists' teaching. In "common use" they find the philosophic name for "almsdeeds." "A man ought not to hold exterior things as his own, but as common to all, that he may portion them out readily to others in time of need." This sentence, an almost literal translation from the Book of Politics, takes on a fuller meaning and is softened by the unselfishness of Christ when it is found in the Summa Theologica of Aquinas.

Let us take boldly the passage from St. Thomas in which he lays down the law of almsgiving.

(2a, 2ae, 32, 5.) "Since love of one's neighbour is commanded us, it follows that everything without which that love cannot be preserved, is also commanded us. But it is essential to the love of one's neighbour, not merely to wish him well, but to act well towards him; as says St. John (1 Ep. 3), 'Let us not love in word nor in tongue, but in deed and in truth.' But to wish and to act well towards anyone implies that we should succour him when he is in need, and this is done by almsgiving. Hence almsgiving is a matter of precept. But because precepts are given in things that concern virtuous living, the almsgiving here referred to must be of such a kind as shall promote virtuous living. That is to say, it must be consonant with right reason; and this in turn implies a twofold consideration, namely, from the point of view of the giver, and from that of the receiver. As regards the giver, it must be noted that what is given should not be necessary to him, as says St. Luke 'That which is superfluous, give in alms.' And by 'not necessary' I mean not only to himself (i.e. what is over and above his individual needs), but to those who depend on him. For a man must first provide for himself and those of whom he has the care, and can then succour such of the rest as are necessitous--that is, such as are without what their personal needs entail. For so, too, nature provides that nutrition should be communicated first to the body, and only secondly to that which is to be begotten of it. As regards the receiver, it is required that he should really be in need, else there is no reason for alms being given him. But since it is impossible for one man to succour all who are in need, he is only under obligation to help such as cannot otherwise be provided for. For in this case the words of Ambrose become applicable: 'Feed them that are dying of starvation, else shall you be held their murderer.' Hence it is a matter of precept to give alms to whosoever is in extreme necessity. But in other cases (namely, where the necessity is not extreme) almsgiving is simply a counsel, and not a command."(Ad 2m.) "Temporal goods which are given a man by God are his as regards their possession, but as regards their use, if they should be superfluous to him, they belong also to others who may be provided for out of them. Hence St. Basil says: 'If you admit that God gave these temporal goods to you, is God unjust in thus unequally distributing His favours? Why should you abound, and another be forced to beg, unless it is intended thereby that you should merit by your generosity, and he by his patience? For it is the bread of the starving that you cling to; it is the clothes of the naked that hang locked in your wardrobe; it is the shoes of the barefooted that are ranged in your room; it is the silver of the needy that you hoard. For you are injuring whoever is in want.' And Ambrose repeats the same thing."

Here it will be noticed that we find the real meaning of those words about a man's duty of portioning out readily to another's use what belongs to himself. It is the correlative to the right to private property.

But a second quotation must be made from another passage closely following on the preceding:

"There is a time when to withhold alms is to commit mortal sin. Namely, when on the part of the receiver there is evident and urgent necessity, and he does not seem likely to be provided for otherwise, and when on the part of the giver he has superfluities of which he has not any probable immediate need. Nor should the future be in question, for this would be looking to the morrow, which the Master has forbidden (Matt. 6)."

(Ibid., 32, 6.) "But 'superfluous' and 'necessity' are to be interpreted according to their most probable and generally accepted meaning. 'Necessary' has two meanings. First, it implies something without which a thing cannot exist. Interpreted in this sense, a man has no business to give alms out of what is necessary to him; for example, if a man has only enough wherewith to feed himself and his sons or others dependent on him. For to give alms out of this

132

would be to deprive himself and his of very life, unless it were indeed for the sake of prolonging the life of someone of extreme importance to Church and State. In that case it might be praiseworthy to expose his life and the lives of others to grave risk, for the common good is to be preferred to our own private interests. Secondly, 'necessary' may mean that without which a person cannot be considered to uphold becomingly his proper station, and that of those dependent on him. The exact measure of this necessity cannot be very precisely determined, as to how far things added may be beyond the necessity of his station, or things taken away be below it. To give alms, therefore, out of these is a matter not of precept, but of counsel. For it would not be right to give alms out of these, so as to help others, and thereby be rendered unable to fulfil the obligations of his state of life. For no one should live unbecomingly. Three exceptions, however, should be made. First, when a man wishes to change his state of life. Thus it would be an act of perfect virtue if a man, for the purpose of entering a religious order, distributed to the poor for Christ's sake all that he possessed. Secondly, when a man gives alms out of what is necessary for his state of life, and yet does so knowing that they can very easily be supplied to him again without much personal inconvenience. Thirdly, when some private person, still more when the State itself, is in the gravest need. In these cases it would be most praiseworthy for a man to give what seemingly was required for the upkeep of his station in life in order to provide against some far greater need."

From these passages it will be possible to construct the theory in vogue during the whole of the Middle Ages. The landholder was considered to possess his property on a system of feudal tenure, and to be obliged thereby to certain acts of suit and service to his immediate lord, or eventually to the King. But besides these burdens which the responsibility of possession entailed, there were others incumbent on him, because of his brotherhood with all Christian folk. He owed a debt, not merely to his superiors, but also to his equals. Such was the interpretation of Christ's commandment which the mediaeval theologians adopted. With one voice they declare that to give away to the needy what is superfluous is no act of charity, but of justice. St. Jerome's words were often quoted: "If thou hast more than is necessary for thy food and clothing, give that away, and consider that in thus acting thou art but paying a debt" (Epist. 50 ad Edilia q. i.); and those others of St. Augustine, "When superfluities are retained, it is the property of others which is retained" (in Psalm 147). These and like sayings of the Fathers constitute the texts on which the moral economic doctrine of what is called the Scholastic School is based. Albertus Magnus (vol. iv. in Sent. 4, 14, p. 277, Lyons, 1651) puts to himself the question whether to give alms is a matter of justice or of charity, and the answer which he makes is compressed finally into this sentence: "For a man to give out of his superfluities is a mere act of justice, because he is rather the steward of them for the poor than the owner." St. Thomas Aquinas is equally explicit, as another short sentence shall show (2a, 2ae, 66, 2, ad 3m): "When Ambrose says 'Let no one call his own that which is common property,' he is referring to the use of property. Hence he adds: 'Whatever a man possesses above what is necessary for his sufficient comfort, he holds by violence.'" And the same view could be backed by quotations from Henry of Ghent, Duns Scotus, St. Bonaventure, the sermons of

Wycliff, and almost every writer of any consequence in that age.

Perhaps to us this decided tone may appear remarkable, and even ill-considered. But it is evident that the whole trouble lies in the precise meaning to be attached to the expressions "superfluous" and "needy." And here, where we feel most of all the need of guidance, it must be confessed that few authors venture to speak with much definiteness. The instance, indeed, of a man placed in extreme necessity, all quote and explain in nearly identical language. Should anyone be reduced to these last circumstances, so as to be without means of subsistence or sufficient wealth to acquire them, he may, in fact must, take from anywhere whatever suffices for his immediate requirements. If he begs for the necessities of life, they cannot be withheld from him. Nor is the expression "necessities of life" to be interpreted too nicely. Says Albertus Magnus: "I mean by necessary not that without which he cannot live, but that also without which he cannot maintain his household, or exercise the duties proper to his condition" (loc. cit., art. 16, p. 280). This is a very generous interpretation of the phrase, but it is the one pretty generally given by all the chief writers of that period. Of course they saw at once that there were practical difficulties in the way of such a manner of acting. How was it possible to determine whether such a one was in real need or not? And the only answer given was that, if it was evident that a man was so placed, there could be no option about giving; almsdeeds then became of precept. But that, if there were no convincing signs of absolute need, then the obligation ceased, and almsgiving, from a command, became a counsel.

In an instance of this extreme nature it is not difficult to decide, but the matter becomes perilously complicated when an attempt is made to gauge the relative importance of "need" and "superfluity" in concrete cases. How much "need" must first be endured before a man has a just claim on another's superfluity? By what standard are "superfluities" themselves to be judged? For it is obvious that when the need among a whole population is general, things possessed by the richer classes, which in normal circumstances might not have been considered luxuries, instantly become such. However then the words are taken, however strictly or laxly interpreted, it must always be remembered that the terms used by the Scholastics do not really solve the problem. They suggest standards, but do not define them, give names, but cannot tell us their precise meaning.

Should we say, then, that in this way they had failed? It is not in place in a book of this kind to sit in judgment on the various theories quoted, and test them to see how far they hold good, or to what extent they should be disregarded, for it is the bare recital of mere historic views which can be here considered. The object has been simply to tell what systems were thought out and held, without attempting to apprize them or measure their value, or point out how far they are applicable to modern times. But in this affair of almsdeeds it is perhaps well to note that the Scholastics could make this much defence of their vagueness. In cases of this kind, they might say, we are face to face with human nature, not as an abstract thing, but in its concrete personal existence. The circumstances must therefore differ in each single instance. General laws can be laid down, but only on the distinct understanding that they are mere principles of direction--in other words, that they are nothing more than general laws. The Scholastics, the mediaeval writers of every school, except a few of that Manichean brood of sects, admitted the necessity of almsgiving. They looked on it from a moral point of view as a high virtue, and from an economic standpoint as a correlative to their individualistic ideas on private property. The one without the other would be unjust. Alone, they would be unworkable; together, mutually independent, they would make the State a fair and perfect thing.

But to fix the exact proportion between the two terms, they held to be the duty of the individual in each case that came to his notice. To give out of a man's superfluities to the needy was, they held, undoubtedly a bounden duty. But they could make no attempt to apprize in definite language what in the receiver was meant by need, and in the giver by superfluity. They made no pretence to do this, and thereby showed their wisdom, for obviously the thing cannot be done. Yet we must note, last of all, that they drew up a list of principles which shall here be set down, because they sum up in a few sentences the wit of mediaeval economists, their spirit of orderly arrangement, and their unanimous opinion on man's moral obligations.

(I) A man is obliged to help another in his extreme need, even at the risk of grave inconvenience to himself.

(II) A man is obliged to help another who, though not in extreme need, is yet in considerable distress, but not at the risk of grave inconvenience to himself.

(III) A man is not obliged to help another whose necessity is slight, even though the risk to himself should be quite trifling.

In other words, the need of his fellow must be adjusted against the inconvenience to himself. Where the need of the one is great, the inconvenience to the other must at least be as great, if it is to excuse him from the just debt of his alms. His possession of superfluities does not compel him to part with them unless there is some real want which they can be expected to supply. In fine, the mediaevalists would contend that almsgiving, to be necessary, implies two conditions, both concomitant:--

(a) That the giver should possess superfluities.

(b) That the receiver should be in need.

Where both these suppositions are fulfilled, the duty of almsgiving becomes a matter not of charity, but of justice.

BIBLIOGRAPHY

Among the original works by mediaeval writers on economic subjects, which can be found in most of the greater libraries in England, we would place the following:

De Recuperatione Terre Sancte, by Pierre du Bois. Edited by C. V. Langlois in Paris. 1891.

Commentarium in Politicos Aristotelis, by Albertus Magnus. Vol. iv. Lyons. 1651.

Summa Theologica, of St. Thomas Aquinas. This is being translated by the English Dominicans, published by Washborne. London. 1911. But the parts that deal with Aquinas' theories of property, &c., have not yet been published.

De Regimine Principio, probably by Ptolomeo de Lucca. It will be found printed among the works of St. Thomas Aquinas, who wrote the first chapters. The portion here to be consulted is in book iv.

Tractatus de Civili Dominio, by Wycliff, published in four vols. in London. 1885-1904.

Bede Jarrett, O.P., M.A.

Unprinted Works of John Wycliff, edited at Oxford in three vols. 1869-1871.

Fasciculus Zizaniorum and the Chronicon Angliae, both edited in the Roll Series, help in elucidating the exact meaning of Wycliff, and his relation to the insurgents of 1381.

Monarchia, edited by Goldast of Hanover in 1611, gives a collection of fifteenth-century writers, including Ockham, Cesena, Roselli, &c.

Summa Moralis, by St. Antonino of Florence, contains a great deal of economic moralising. But the whole four volumes (Verona, 1740) must be searched for it.

Among modern books which can be consulted with profit are:--

Illustrations of the Mediaeval Thought, by Reginald Lane Poole. 1884. London.

Political Theories of the Middle Ages, by F. W. Maitland. 1900. Cambridge.

History of Mediaeval Political Thought, by A. J. Carlyle. 1903. &c. Oxford (unfinished).

History of English Law, by Pollock and Maitland. 1898. Cambridge.

Introduction to English Economic History, by W. J. Ashley. 1892.   London.

Economie Politique au Moyen Age, by V. Brandts. 1895. Louvain.

La Propriété après St. Thomas, by Mgr. Deploige, Revue   Neo-Scholastique. 1895, 1896. Louvain.

History of Socialism, by Thomas Kirkup. 1909. London.

Great Revolt of 1381, by C. W. C. Oman. 1906. Oxford.

Lollardy and the Reformation, by Gairdner. 1908-1911 (three   vols.) London.

England in the Age of Wycliff, by G. M. Trevelyan. 1909. London.

Leaders of the People, by J. Clayton. 1910. London. A sympathetic   account of Ball, Cade, &c.

Social Organisation, by G. Unwin. 1906. Oxford.

Bede Jarrett, O.P., M.A.

Outlines of Economic History of England, by H. O. Meredith. 1908.   London.

Mutual Aid in a Mediaeval City, by Prince Kropotkin (Nineteenth   Century Review. Vol. xxxvi. p. 198).

INDEX

Made in the USA
Monee, IL
17 December 2020